TRUE FACE
OF LOVE

I0161443

EILEEN CURTEIS

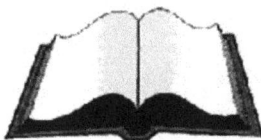

CCB Publishing
British Columbia, Canada

True Face of Love

Copyright ©2023 by Eileen Curteis
ISBN-13   978-1-77143-566-6
First Edition

Library and Archives Canada Cataloguing in Publication
Curteis, Eileen, 1942-, author
True face of love / written by Eileen Curteis. -- First edition.
Issued in print and electronic formats.
ISBN 978-1-77143-566-6 (softcover).--ISBN 978-1-77143-567-3 (PDF)
Additional cataloguing data available from Library and Archives Canada

Cover artwork, as well as all poems, are by Eileen Curteis.

Cover design by Carey Pallister.

Author photo credit: Frances Litman – www.franceslitman.com

Publisher: CCB Publishing
               British Columbia, Canada
               www.ccbpublishing.com

Love one another as I have loved you.
John 15:12

Written for my friends
who travel the journey with me.

Acknowledgements

Carey Pallister, for designing my book cover, for reading my work and acknowledging me as a gifted poet. Susan McCaslin, a well-known poet and author of many books, for her ongoing advice, friendship and encouragement. Jason Curteis, for his insightful and powerful Preface. Judith Miller, for her inspirational Foreword. Thanks also to my wonderful friends who have generously acknowledged my work on the back cover of my book. Paul Rabinovitch, for his expertise and compatibility in publishing a number of my books, including this one.

CONTENTS

POEMS FROM
SOJOURNER KNOW YOURSELF **- 1993** ... 175

POEMS FROM
WIND DAUGHTER - 1998

POEMS FROM

FOREWORD – JUDITH MILLER

Sister Eileen Curteis has been writing and creating original works of art most of her adult life. Her many books take on a life of their own as she draws the reader into her world of imagery through poetry and sketches. In this particular volume of her latest work, the journey she takes you on builds in excitement as she allows you to explore your destiny with hers. Each poem she writes builds on the next, inviting you, the reader, to experience her truth firsthand. Join with me now in reading this exquisite book of literary accomplishment covering a span of forty-seven years.

PREFACE – JASON CURTEIS

It's not often that you get to go on a soul journey with another person. Even rarer still is to be able to witness the evolution of another traveller as they become more fearless in putting themselves out into the world for us to see and to learn from. And it's not enough to just be fearless. To be able to articulate the "true face of love," while at the same time exposing life's sharp edge of grittiness, is more than just a talent. You need to be crushed first in order to grow, and then unwavering, you need to strive for the light, drawn to the mystery we are all being swept into.

Eileen Curteis is a woman at the height of her personal awareness and literary powers. She has become a master of her art. Her voice has evolved through the decades and ten previous books of poetry and artwork in order to arrive here. Now the muse is demanding more, insisting on a greater, deeper truth. She has torn away the last veil of innuendo in her work and laid her experience bare. The sharp writing, bold metaphor, and lovely allusions are still there, along with the emotional gravitas, but her new work is like a beautiful cosmic hammer hitting nail after nail and filling the silence with the sweet sound of truth and strength, over and over again.

I'm already a huge fan of Eileen's work, but I am actually stunned by these new poems. They feel like a gift. Her previous work spoke of struggle, joy, acceptance, perseverance, and awe. The poems evoked a feeling of peace and revelled at the divine song of the universe, and our place in it. That work was amazing, but these new poems, though clearly an evolution of what came before, crackle with power and beauty. They describe the human experience, her experience, like being connected directly to the Source. The language, as always, is evocative, but it's cleaner, electrical, true.

Eileen has told me that when writing these poems she was ready to come out, ready to break the cords and carry the Light. The time spent flourishing underground has enabled her to access the higher gifts. She knows she doesn't have all the answers but like a child of the universe awakening, she knows she's being led. Thankfully, for us, we get to join her in the journey.

INTRODUCTION – EILEEN CURTEIS

I write not for distinction, not for acclaim, not to please another. I write because my soul is on fire with Love, a Love that has burnt its truth into the very core of my being. I write because I want others to explore alongside me the amazing powers of healing that lie within the human spirit. I want you, the reader, to experience a new kind of hope and fullness of life as you read my work and I'm trusting that my poetry can be a vehicle for this to happen.

This is book two of the pandemic, *True Face of Love*. During this time of social distancing, my soul has become so intimate with me that it awakens me during the night, and I hear within myself the infused words that need to be spoken. Given as small kernels through the night, they often become a full-fledged poem the following day.

Whether you name this phenomenon God, Spirit, Other, it is all coming from Source, a Love Force Energy that has been guiding me from the time I was very young. Not always understood for my way of walking, I would sometimes abandon my soul, die in my own tracks and then be driven back to find her.

What my book addresses is a spiritual quest where one's soul, in this particular case mine, had to pass through a journey of annihilation over and over again until the purity it hungered for could be arrived at.

Because of my own profound and often tarnished journey, it is my belief that once a person has tasted exhilaration beyond what any human level can offer, the soul will no longer settle for anything less. Each person's journey will be different and yet, the quest for wholeness will be what indelibly binds us together.

Although this book does not include my work as an artist, it does through its poetry, give a coverage of the evolution of my soul's development through the many years of my wandering yet purposeful life.

The first section of my book includes the new poetry, the pandemic poetry, fully alive with where my human and spiritual journey has and is taking me. With this new poetry, my only remaining desire is that I will continue to be purified in the depths of my soul and that my quest to make God's love known will be more fully realized.

I will now take you back in time to Kamloops, BC, where my gift as a poet was first acknowledged. In 1975 as a Sister of Saint Ann, I was happily engaged as the principal and kindergarten teacher at St. Ann's Academy, when a man named Ian Clark discovered my work as a poet and artist and wanted it to be shared. In that same year, my first book *Risk*, was published by the King's Men, an ecumenical group of Anglican, Roman Catholic and United Church Laymen's Guild. Already contained within that book were the seeds of where my soul would be taking me as a poet and author of a variety of books.

In 1979, I had a ten-month hermitage experience in Ottawa where my one desire was to write poetry, but the well was dry and nothing, but a dribble came. Somewhat perplexed by this experience, I realized I could not push the hand of Spirit and I even doubted whether I would ever write again.

In the early part of that year, I met with Dr. Frank Tierney, a professor of English at Ottawa University and also an editor at Borealis Press. I showed him my work and upon reading it, he assured me that I was a true poet and once again wanted to see my work published. The other editors, however, were not in agreement and so the timing was not right for further publication. However, the gift I received from Dr. Tierney, was the assurance that indeed I was a true poet and that was sufficient for me to continue pursuing my call.

In the springtime of that year, the artist side of me suddenly began seeing visions and I quickly drew them on paper. I felt that my whole life was somehow immersed in the sketches and so, like some kind of a treasure, I held on to them. I then returned to Victoria, BC, where once again I would find myself immersed in a teaching profession.

Only in 1993, thirteen years later, did I return to the Ottawa sketches and my soul was then ready to produce the poetry that would tell the story behind them. This time I would look at my art and instantly the poem would be there. They were healing poems and I knew they would speak to the people I was journeying with. Dennis Steinle and his wife Helen had a printing press in Victoria, and they helped me publish my next book, *Sojourner Know Yourself.*

In 1997, I returned to the remaining sketches that had been given to me in my Ottawa year and once again I knew the story behind them. This time the poetry came quickly along with a brand-new style that was succinct and powerful. I wasn't thinking of publishing my work until another woman poet approached me at Queenswood, our Sister of Saint Ann Retreat Centre in Victoria, BC. Her name was Hannah Main-van der Kamp and she asked if I would share some of my poetry with her. After reading my material she put me in touch with another well-known poet, Susan McCaslin living in Langley, BC. They both agreed that my work needed to be published and directed me to Richard Olafson of Ekstasis Editions, in Victoria, BC, who published *Moving On* in 1997. It was this kind of assurance I needed in order to go more public with my work.

In 1998, I was ready for another publication, and I titled the book, *Wind Daughter*. Once again, I was in touch with Dr. Frank Tierney from Ottawa University who kindly wrote the preface for this book and Richard Olafson of Ekstasis Editions published it with photography and poetry intermingled.

In 2001, Hillside Printing published *Dance of the Mystic Healer*. The poetry in this book was enhanced by my artistic sketches which were reproduced in black and white rather than in their original colour. This time the poetry flowed in rhyming verses with a lyrical style.

In 2007, Ekstasis Editions published *Face of a Gypsy* with photography and poetry. Susan McCaslin who had become both a good friend and mentor offered to provide a preface to accompany this book.

In 2008, I had already discovered the right publisher for my ongoing work, Paul Rabinovitch, from CCB Publishing in Terrace, BC. Besides producing a quality book, Paul also offered to do the marketing of it.

Because of my full-time healing ministry, my time for writing became limited and in a literary way I preferred to be in the background as much as possible. Other books were published in the intervening years through CCB Publishing but I have chosen not to include the poetry from these books.

In 2018, I felt with the publication of my book of *Exposed,* art, poetry and prose, that I had arrived at a pivotal point and wouldn't be producing anything further. Unbeknownst to me, the surprise of the pandemic was that the best of my work was yet to come.

Beginning on May 2, 2020, for the next 70 days and 70 nights, seventy poems and seventy sketches arrived at my door. I titled that book, *Walk With Me Into the Light.* I then had a month's respite where nothing came and then the poetry began flowing again. This time I felt an invitation deep within me to share not only my new poems but other poems through the years, many of which are no longer in print.

I trust that the gift of my God-given poetry will speak to you and will bless and heal you in the same way that it has blessed and healed me.

COVID POEMS

2020 - 2022

THE NEW EARTH

Some of us began singing
the unknown song
the world had been waiting for.

On that day
the world opened its doors
and windows
and the breeze
came blowing through.

Church bells rang blissfully
in the sky
announcing the freedom to worship
anywhere at any time
on bended knee.

Political systems died gracefully
in the luxurious lap of God
who loved everyone
no matter
what race or colour or creed.

And the feet of old women and men
came prancing down the street
with children by their side.

And the sun shone
in a way
it had never
shone before.

DESTINED FOR THE HIGH SEAS

Grappling
with thick fog
and going nowhere in it
I have become
my own best navigator.

No longer living
in a sinking ship
I've moved into
a season called favourable.

Even the winds
and the tides
have shifted for me.

Floating
in free waters
I go
wherever the current goes.

Holding back nothing
I'm a circular soul
destined
for the high seas.

Taking hold
of the rudder of my life
Someone
is doing the steering
for me.

WHEN LOVE BURSTS YOU OPEN

Hiding
her own blood
the speechless one
bit her tongue
down to nothing.

Hunting
for something good
oppression
drove her to find it.

This time
a sword shoved down
the wrong way
could have killed her.

But Love
knew
otherwise.

Overwhelmed
by her goodness
the oppressed one
sank deep down
into it.

It was not the first time
Love burst her open
nor would it be
the last.

LET LOVE SPARKLE

There's nothing romantic
about tasting
your own bile
and have it go down
the wrong way.

Reversal means
holding your heart high
not
way down low.

It means
stop
befriending your enemy
the muddy one
inside you.

Splash yourself clean
have a good bath
until it makes you pure
from the inside-out.

People will love
your sparkling self
and you will too.

You're neither an angel
nor a saint
but truly
there is a goodness in you.

SELF LOVE

Standing
on a pedestal
I fell down flat.

Wanting recognition
pride
was the tricky monster
pumping me up
the wrong way.

Embarrassment
like pinched skin
left me feeling
uncomfortable.

As for my ego
it died
on the way down.

Picking up
the remains
of my selfhood
I grew to love her
as she was.

No longer dreaming
of a castle in the sky
I know now
my true home
lives within me.

EFFERVESCENT LOVE

Just yesterday
I saw something
more radiant
than devastation
sitting beside me.

Clasping her hand
in mine
it was the face
of a woman
I knew so well.

My own ragged face
somewhat wrinkled
in time
casting light
over the place
where darkness
dwells.

Her smile
encompassed me
like an unseen world
I was being drawn into.

Effervescent
was her love
and I
stepped into it.

NEW SELF

Battered, broken
beaten down
I've tasted the dregs
of my former self
my lowly self.

Today is a new day
and all that is good
beautiful
lovely in me
I shall claim it
as my own.

As for my old self
my dying self
I shall treat her
like a royal queen
for her essence
is indeed lovely.

She is wise
beyond all telling.

And like the fresh dew
of the morning air
she reminds me
I am older now
and in many ways
younger.

NOBILITY

Too soft, too squishy
too flat, too hard
the time is long overdue
to climb out of
your marshmallow existence.

Whether it be
a soft pillow
or hard one
you lie on
neither is right for you.

Even the clean sheets
on a therapeutic bed
leave you feeling messy
on the inside.

What you need
is to speak your truth
and leave the residue
of falsity behind.

Picking up
the shredded pieces
of your shattered heart
grow to love yourself
the way you are.

Let nobility
come shining through.

TRUE PERFORMER

When harshness
hits you in the face
pick up your instrument
and play your music well.

Let go of adulation
and know
the jarring notes
of a song writer
is where you must begin.

Pleasing an audience
with happy notes
when it's a sad song
you want to sing
will get you nowhere.

Similarly
pushing the wild side
of you down
when it wants
to come roaring out
will end up defeating you.

Stop targeting
yourself:
Come out of the closet
and sing
what you need to sing!

THE SOUL'S COMPASS

Stabbed to death
I am the guttered out one
who said:
"Who put this knife through me?"

Like a nightmare
gone wild
too high a level of sensitivity
can do that to you.

Steady your soul now
let the energy
of your bouncing heart
calm down.

Be wise.
Be still.
Watch
how the current flows
and follow its lead.

Without judging anyone
take hold
of the reins of your life
and don't let the false finger
of another
point you in the wrong direction.

From now on
follow the compass
of your soul.

WATERFALL OF GOD

The paradox is this:
When Love
burns a hole in your heart
you want more of it.

It's the empty part
of you
longing to be filled.

Thirsting
for Love
it's the heat
of the fire in you.

Each day
the spark of it
grows bigger
and bigger.

I suppose
you could compare it
to water
and say:
An oasis of hope
is gurgling up
within me.

Quenching my thirst
if this be God
I shall go on
drinking it in.

NOBODY BECOMES SOMEBODY

Little nobody
wanting to be somebody
why bury your grief
in a body
too small to carry it?

Pushing your tears down
too far down
makes only
a trickle of water
come through.

Yes, little nobody,
the truth is this:
A hard mass of cement
has grown up within you.

Too much anguish
under that sweet smile of yours
so why bury your tears
when an explosion of them
could set you free.

Grief
is the wounded ogre
in you.

Stand up
and claim it
as your own.

OLD WISE SOUL

I'm an abandoned soul
grappling
with thick fog
and going nowhere in it.

Losing my way
before finding it
I am like an infant
newborn.

Clean
clear
spotless.

Stunted
at birth
I am an old soul
grown young again.

Meanness
violence
torture
nothing
can disturb me now.

Even the slivers
in the skin
of my soul
know this
to be true.

BECOMING THE NEW BREED

Small creatures
hidden away
in the dark corners
of our hurting mind.

Little paupers
closing our mouths shut
before
the tongue
gets opened wide.

Heralding in
a new voice
with ecstasy
in it.

Standing
in lowliness
so we can sing
the High notes
well.

The God-given music
of a lifetime
we've been waiting for.

Sing it we must
lest we die
in the old tracks
of our former selves.

LET LOVE REIGN

I am an adult woman
returning to the innocence
of my birth
the time when I knew nothing
of what I know now.

Going backwards in time
I knew
God's womb
was bigger
than my mother's womb.

An all-knowing place
more expansive
than anything
I could have imagined.

There was no jailing-up
of souls here.

Saint and sinner alike
saw
what the majesty of God
looked like.

Anything less than Love
got crumpled
into the dust.

And even the dead souls
came back to life.

THE BOOK OF MY LIFE

I was the small girl at school
who said:
"You think you know me
but you read me
like an unread book."

From then on I became
sweet, kind, loveable
with something nagging me
on the inside.

I was too young then
to know about the snake
the dark side of life
festering in me.

Years later
I pushed myself up
out of the dreary dungeon
I had been living in.

Instead of wearing
black socks
I came out
wearing white.

Happily closing
one chapter of my life
I was ready now
for the next.

BEACON OF LIGHT

Dark emotions
are tricky creatures
that rattle you
on the inside.

They know
how to sharpen up
a blunt knife
and get you
twisted in.

In the underground world
they are the secret navigators
known
for their deviousness.

Just when you think
you have a clean slate
they dip
their dagger in.

Be brave
be wary of them
and if need be
carry them
to the Light.

You
are your own
best beacon.

AUTUMN VIGOUR

Like the insistent noise
of mosquitoes in your head
harsh words live there
as long as you let them.

Turning nasty words inward
they will soon turn
clean water into scum.

Now turn yourself outward
and ask the seasons:
How can I do things differently?

Noted for their intelligence
they will tell you:
Each season has a purpose
so choose the one
that will invigorate you.

Deliberately
air out your lungs
and feel
the crisp fresh breeze
of the Autumn air
go circulating through you.

Now crunching your own leaves
red, yellow, green and brown,
put new colour
into the life you live.

MOTHER LOVE SAYS

when you stop
clutching my breast
the milk you desire
will flow freely.

It will be creamy soft
and the taste
will be delectable.

Be you a man
a woman
a child,
stop decimating
my Name
and you will know
the gift
that is mine
to give.

You will drink it down
like pure fluid
and it will restore you
in your hour of need.

Anything limited
will become limitless
and even
the gluttonous
shall go on
drinking more.

READ ME

Eavesdropping
I heard my friend say:
When I try too hard
my life is nothing more
than the torn-up page
of a book.

Even
when I have something
good to say
people read me
the wrong way.

Sometimes
I go to the library
and people find me
sitting on an empty shelf.

No longer hidden away
they pick me up
and dust me off.

I am a small word
but to them
I am big.

Magnanimous now
we sit in a circle
and read each other
the right way.

STILL POINT

Life had become
a racing machine
and I
went panting after it.

Had I been
a dog, a cat
chasing my tail
it might have been
different.

But I am human
with two feet
on a treadmill
I cannot stop.

Racing
toward a finish line
I never get to
my body
wears itself out.

Drastic as it is
it's the wake-up call
that turns me inward.

No longer zooming
around my head
something like still air
enters me now.

BEAUTY OF A SCARRED SOUL

Deceptively sweet
she hid herself away
until the dark side
of her face appeared
with daggers in it.

Like a razor
something
was cutting her up
on the inside.

Some say
it was betrayal
of a loved one.

Others felt
the wound
went deeper.

No one knew
for sure
what the scream
of a scarred soul
looks like.

Only she
who gave birth
to herself
could capture the ache
of something beautiful.

HEALING THE TORN HEART

My name is Baby
and I came into our world
loving it
the way I should.

I lived
with a good family
and grew up
as best I could
until one day
someone
used their scissors
and cut me up
the wrong way.

From then on
I knew:
If blood
can make you bleed
my heart
had done it to me.

Years later
I listened
to my bruised skin
and she told me:
Hiding the tear
will not heal you
exposing it
will.

REFRAMING GOD'S NAME

You don't like God's name do you
because punishment
was drilled into you
the wrong way.

Why not look at God differently
spell the name backwards
and see what you get:
a loveable, four-legged creature
licking your kind face
and telling you
how good you are.

Delightful as this is
you're living
in a mongrel world
where angry dogs
sometimes called humans
can devour you.

Hiding in a kennel
won't do it:
Look outwards
to a Love
vaster than you are.

Choose God
and put a new name
on top of the old one.

POLLYANNA THE REALIST

My name is Pollyanna
and I'm sitting
on the porch
of my friend's home.

It's a sunny day
where people revere me
and I'm revelling in it.

Night comes
and I return home
to the wrinkled-up
part of me.

It's the grumpy side
of my sunny self
I keep hidden
under lock and key.

In my night-time dreams
the enemy
I am to myself
pounces on me
and tells me
it's OK to be me.

"Miss Pollyanna"
she says:
"You will not thrive
until you become real."

EVOLUTION

Grumpy weed
turning into
perky flower
with a new look
I hadn't planned on.

Standing upright
in my garden
of honeysuckle
it's God
who put me here.

Relishing my life as it is
I will outgrow myself
and exuberant species
different than I am
will get planted
beside me.

Born of ethereal Energy
they will come
with breathtaking vitality.

Without
bumping me over
they will honour
how the old path
gets blended
with the new.

SOUL MATES

Mesmerized
by two faces in one
that's how I got to know you.

Presenting yourself
as a beam of light
I felt singled out
as if your soul
had entered mine.

Your dark eyes
beguiled me
like the stars of night.

Peering into them
I loved what I saw
and like a flame of fire
it glowed within me.

Your skin was soft and pure
and even the touch of it
against mine
was something
I could revel in.

Treasuring
the wonder of you
I held the fragility
of your small hands in mine
and named you God incarnate.

HOROSCOPE READING

Beautiful heart
serene and pure
that's the way
you entered our world.

Pitching a tent here
your small body
fell into a deep pit
you couldn't climb out of
and yet you did.

A nomad wanderer
you were
lost in the turmoil
of a world
too big for you.

And yet,
like a fragile bird
fluttering
your flattened wings
outward,
we watched you grow
resilient
in times of despair.

A faith journeyer you were
believing in a horoscope
that had black lines
running through it.

ECSTATIC HEART

Love
was the magnet
you were drawn into.

Wooed early
you left everything behind
family, friends
to follow
the call
of your soul.

Even in betrayal
when hurt
cut you open
like a sword
you followed
your call.

Love was bigger
stronger
than the blade
of a knife
going into you.

Even in abandonment
you came out
of your ordeal
more alive
than had you never
gone in.

RESILIENT KEY

Silver shining
beautiful key
you opened
my locked door
and I let you in.

More than a friend
you were a teacher
to me.

Holding up
a cracked mirror
you showed me
the dark side of shame.

Next came a portrait
vibrant and alive
with the new me in it.

Face radiant
unwrinkled
and smooth.

"Oh key," I said:
"You raised me high
when I had shrunk
down low
and in its place
you gave me hope
that I might live."

INNER TRANSFORMATION

I suppose
I could have been
a kind atheist
but I grew up
wanting to be Christ's girl,
wanting to be good,
perhaps too good.

Living
in my estranged body
I took the gospel
seriously.

Wanting
the grain of wheat
to die
I bombed myself out early
that I might live.

Picking up the dregs
of my disintegrated self
I grew to love her
as she was.

No longer
puffed up
or elated
I came to know
the deep down
quiet me.

SPOTLIGHT IN A GRAVEYARD

The conundrum is this:
I am the unhappy
happy one
standing in a cemetery
of my own making.

Camouflaging myself
a temper tantrum child
am I.

Rebellious
and reluctantly admitting,
earth school
is a slapping machine
I dislike going into.

Even the gospel of truth
I love so dearly
has torn pages in it.

Perhaps now
I should add my own name
to the Bible and say:
In every flawed life
there is a trail of goodness.

In the end
it's the spotlight
in the dark
I will be remembered by.

RECHARGING MY ENERGY

Hiding the place
where the crucifix went in
I pretended to be happy
when I wasn't.

Concealing my true face
I functioned
supposedly well
in a society
that never knew me.

I was not a Jesus person
but inside my soul
was a gash
that reminded me of Him.

If it was Love
this Man had
I wanted it.

Opening myself up
I felt the splurge
of something beautiful.

Not my energy but His
recharging me
like a new-found battery
and I went dancing
through the potholes
of my soul.

LIVING IN MYSTERY

It was as if the talking bird
had a language
all her own.

Tearing around like a mad woman
there was something sneaky
and quiet about her.
She knew things others didn't.

Was she a bird, a dog, a rabbit
in a past life
or maybe a moon or star
in the planetary system?

No one really knew
and yet,
perched on the fence
of our world
she left us wondering.

To find out who she was
she sat down with God
and asked:
"Who am I?"

God answered:
"It's not for you to know
the Mystery of existence
or pre-existence.
Just be glad and revel in it."

AN ORDINARY SOUL

The once wise virgin
turned into a jack-in-the-box
whose whirling energy
got out of control.

In her ignorance
she jumped up high
and got pushed down low.

Feeling foolish
as much as she wanted
the best in life
she found it difficult
to get there.

One day
she said to her soul:
"Sit down at the kitchen sink
and learn your lessons
the hard way.

Scrub out the stains
of your too perfect self
and try being ordinary.

Now walk over
to the dinner table
and tell pride
slumped over a chair
it's okay to be you."

NESTING TIME

Floating in clean water
white swan
with a regal demeanour
gave birth to her babies
and I was one of them.

A tiny creature malformed
I did not like
my inherited disposition.

Sometimes dismissed
as the cranky awkward one
I would float backwards
down stream.

One day
I left the pond of my birth
and came floating out
to the wide-open sea.

Spreading my wings
outward
there was nothing
disjointed in me.

No longer anonymous to myself
I was the smallest of the small birds
who left home
to find the nest
that was right for me.

A FULL-FLEDGED LIFE

Delicious
is no longer a word
in my vocabulary.

Too much frustration
bottled up
for too long a time
has exploded
within me.

Like splintered glass
am I
and injured
because of it.

Standing in the raw
I swear to God
this is my own
pretty bruised up face
not pretty at all.

Reduced to nothing
I called it
the new word of God
forming in me.

No longer baffled
by a dainty life
I've entered
a full-fledged one.

PERENNIAL BLOOM

Riddled in silence
I am the gentle
strong one
wanting to speak
but cannot.

Strapped down
in a chair
you ignore me
push me over
until the whimper in me
becomes a shout.

Finding the exit door
I go whizzing past you
into a night
that can no longer
confine my day.

Discovering
a new garden
to live in
I give birth
to a perennial bloom.

I grow
I flourish
I become the person
God made me to be.

BIRTHING OF THE HIGHER SELF

In every good life
there's a skeleton
tucked inside your shoe.

Bouncing along happily
she sleeps there
until the day
you bump into
something hard:
a concrete wall
or iron gate
you can't get through.

Stymied at last
if you haven't met
the embryo
of the feisty one
living in you
you'll meet her now.

Her love is staggering:
She wants
what she wants
new warmth
on anything cold
or hard within you.

Rise up
and meet her now.

HOLY FIRE

If truth be made known
a lie detector
on my tongue
will tell it to you.

On the shady side
of my face
appearance
is deceiving.

I shift, I change
I turn the mirror
backwards
I see out
no one sees in.

An enigma to myself
and to many
I sit, I stand, I stare
at the cold arena of life.

Shivering
for heat to come in
I find it
in the last flame
of my burnt-out self.

I am at one now
with the Fire
in me.

SCHOOL LIFE

Not all children thrive
and I happened
to be one of them.

At school
I was the stiff girl
the backward girl.

Jumbled up words
left me feeling
inadequate.

Other children
were exhilarated
by the challenge
of learning.

More knowledgeable than I
they answered questions
at a speed foreign to me.

Nervous and fearful
the word dumb
got implanted in my brain.

Years later
I became a teacher
and reached out
to all children
especially the ones
who resembled me.

THE ART OF BECOMING

Worshipping
the talents of others
she forgot about
her own true ones.

Becoming smaller
than she was
she went around
like a pouting child.

If nothing else
could change her
the handle
of an axe would.

The cut went deep
so deep
that the blood
ran red.

Out she came
beautiful as a fluffy chick
bursting through
the shell of an egg.

Waltzing down the street
no one questioned her behaviour
she just was who she was
and the town's folk
grew to loving her that way.

MYSTERIOUS ENERGY

You can't put soul Energy
in a box
she's too big for that.

Her parameters
extend
far beyond the earth.

She lives and thrives
in open spaces
and if you try
placing her in a room
with blockades in it
she will not enter.

Moving quickly
and quietly
through the corridors
of time
she is never noisy
but when she finds
someone on her radar line
they can converse
for days
weeks, months, years.

Deep
and mysterious
is the world
they plunge into.

LET MY WINGS SOAR

Fragile
as a white lily
growing in me
I want to become
what I want
to become.

Having known
the hard prick
of cactus
I shall not
return there.

Beyond me
is the field
I have not seen
but am walking toward.

When I get there
I will surprise myself
and say:
Like irrigation am I
and greener
because of it.

On that day
the bent wings
of my chastened heart
will go soaring free.

YOU LIGHT ME UP

Barnacled in
and barnacled out
I know
what despair
feels like.

Running
from her
she chased after me
with a weapon
I did not like.

An inward gun
blasting
the darkness
out of me.

Dead
as dead
could be
I needed a battery
to recharge me
a current of Light
with radiance
in it.

And so You came
flashing
Your brightness
into me.

BURNT LOVE

Aching to be seen
and choosing to be not
the tooth of loneliness
gnawed its way into me.

Isolating myself
from others
and too shy
to make myself
known
I put a hood
over my head.

Living separately
in a shell
that needed
to be cracked open
I took a hammer to it.

No longer
an observer of life
I plunged into it
headlong.

Tasting
my own burnt skin
I grew to love
the hardship
that today
has made me whole.

CANDELABRA OF LIGHT

I go sauntering
through the world
wearing
my mask of anguish
backwards.

Others
go sauntering
with me.

Like crumpled-up
pieces of paper
thrown into the garbage
we choose not
to dishonour ourselves
that way.

Even in the darkest
of alleys
we've grown to love
the light
that is in us.

Loving ourselves
the way we are
we see
how the candelabra
of our lives
has led us together.

VISIONARY WOMAN

Wisdom
old crone
withered up one
inside me
dancing freely
over a barbed wire fence.

No longer
starved for affection
I've left
the frivolous life
behind.

Exchanging
my old heart
for the new one
real love
doesn't leave
my tongue
dripping dry.

My soul creates
its own stilts
and what you see
is what you get.

A tall world
without
the word small
entangled in it.

PROVIDENTIAL HAND

Innocent and naive
life became a hornet
chasing me
down the street
stinging me
in all the wrong places
so I could learn
my lessons well.

Smart, dumb
ignorant, brilliant
I was all these things
and nothing
could satisfy me.

Craving to be loved
Providence spotted
the hole in my heart
and placed
her lush finger
over it.

Fully satisfied
my aimless wandering
ceased.

The hornet
became a honey bee
and I
drank of her nectar.

HOLY PURE ONE

God
is free flowing
nothing stiff
within her.

You and she
are one.

Bouncing over
too many stringent rules
she's the effortless one
rising in you.

The trickster
reminding you
not to point your finger
at another
when it's your own dirt
you need to see.

Breathtakingly beautiful
she comes quietly
hiddenly
cleaning the cobwebs
out of you.

She's the purest
of the pure ones
and her name is
God with us.

BIG LOVE BECKONS YOU

Make no mistake
about it
the kiss
of a flirting bird
is for real
and if it lands on you
you will know it
when it comes.

It doesn't matter
if you preen
your feathers
this way or that
She's not interested
in your looks.

It's the temperature
in your heart
that matters.

Are you hot
or are you cold?
Are you open
or are you shut?

And even
if you're not ready
She will wait
until you are.

UNCOVERING THE TRUTH

Truth
cannot tell a lie
and so
my story gets told.

Happiest
in my alone space
I am the introverted one
wanting to speak
but cannot.

A veil
hangs over my face
and I hide behind it.

Extroverts hold the floor
speak eloquently
and I listen attentively.

Blushing my way
out of the room
with nothing to say
I know
what ignorance
and diminishment
feel like.

Returning home
I regain my dignity.
I am who I am.

BRANCHING OUT

For too long now
I've been living
the Miss Proper life.

I'm not potentially
dangerous
but push me
underground
and I will explode.

Neither
is my nature radical
but put me in a square box
and I'll squirm my way out.

I'm at a crossroad now:
Either I go backward
and die
or move forward
and live.

Risking
the crooked road
over the straight one
sterility
is no longer
an option for me.

It's the unknown path
I'm being called to.

WARRIOR WOMAN

Blind eyes
falling into a deep pit
I couldn't get out of.

Groping around
in the dark
I lost my soul
to find it.

Taking my cold
clammy hand
in Yours
You kindled
a fire in me.

Springing upward
and galloping along
the way a horse does
the zest of love
grew strong
within me.

Leaping
over obstacles
I surmounted them
the way a warrior would.

A late bloomer
am I
coming into my own.

GNARLED BEAUTY

Too complex
to know myself fully
I fell prey
to the enemy within.

The sinister one
who got flipped over
early
by the dark side
of life.

The crooked one
who saw
what the crushed ego
of a smooth face
turned jagged
looks like.

The multi-faceted one
who let
disgruntlement in
so jubilation
would follow.

The twisted one
who chose
to have a gnarled look
as if the beauty
of her tree
depended on it.

A WINTERIZED SOUL

When a sweet thing
turns sour
your hour
will be at hand.

Until then
be the butterfly you are
flirting around
with the kiss of God saying:
happy, happy am I.

For survival
your soul needs this
so don't put a damper
on love.

Soon enough
ready or not
a nightmare
will come upon you.

Slamming
the sweet door shut
there will be nothing feeble
in the love
you harness.

Winterizing yourself
it's the wild woman's
reckless journey inward.

ETERNALLY YOURS

Universal One
multi-faceted kaleidoscope
of my being
and all other beings too.

Take me as I am
wrinkled-up
illiterate
in my knowledge
of You.

Shape my world big
loosen
anything small
anything
not born
of the grandeur
of You.

Let me sip
and splurge
until the whole of me
becomes ensconced
in the whole of You.

I am Yours
today
tomorrow
and forever.

BOUNCE YOUR BALL UPWARD

Be strong, be brave
swallow your tears
and be told
not to cry again.

It's the photograph
of your early self
a sick mermaid
lovely on the outside
but disintegrating
from within.

Now visit
your true self
and tell love
not to treat you
that way.

From now on
whoever you are
whoever you be
bounce your ball
upward
not downward.

Sing, dance
paint, write
twirl your baton
as if your life
depended on it.

REDEEM YOUR CHILD

Sloppy tears
on the face of a child
can redeem you now.

Reminiscing
is healthy
so take your book down
from the shelf
and read your life
into it.

Take your child
by the hand
and tell her:
"It's OK
to be a tiny pea
in a pod.

It could be
the most delectable
part of you
the fleshy part
that got pushed
under.

Taste yourself
know yourself
love yourself
eat only
what is good for you."

BEAUTY OF A BARREN TREE

A stripped-down tree
am I
naked
so naked
you can see
right through me now.

Leaves gone
hurled
into the wind.

Branches broken
limbs twisted
the torn-up part of me
shattered to the ground.

Juicy fruit
dried up
wizened into nothing.

No more pretense here
no more defending myself
trying to be something
I am not.

Stripped to the ground
the bony ground
I come out of this wilderness
more beautiful
than had I never gone in.

MADE IN GOD'S IMAGE

Snowdrops
pure white
lily-white
that's the way
we came into
Your world
sparkling clean
like the first snowfall
of winter.

Our small bodies
exquisitely formed
teeth, mouth, nose
eyes, ears
fragile beings
perfectly formed
in the likeness of You.

And, yet,
when treated wrongly
like China cups
we chip easily.

Therefore
be kind
as God is kind.

Handle us gently
lest we die
before we live.

TRANSPARENCY
OF A CLEAN WINDOW

Dirt on the window
grub on the floor
sometimes
stagnation
is what you need
to stand in.

Swallowing hurt
is like sitting
on a hard chair
with the ache
of disappointment
in you.

This time
no one
can loosen
the scab
only you can.

Come out
from hiding
and let the pus
flow free.

Now take a cloth
to your window
and scrub it clean.

JOURNEY OF THE HEART

When life
slaps me in the face
I don't dwell
on the tragedy
of it.

I just say
to myself:
Each day
is different
a bruise, a sore
a joy, a hope.

Some say:
That's the chore
of being human
pushing your body
up a hill
when you would rather
be going down.

Others say:
Stamina
is the new melody
in your heart.

Treat her well
and she
will go on
singing to you.

EVOLUTIONARY CHRISTMAS PRESENT
2021

Corona virus
harsh teacher
global teacher
spunky piece of matter.

Like a blast
in the night
you came
you wielded
your sword.

Purging us out
you cut through
our smugness
and we did not
like it.

Stymied by life
we could not resist
your coming
your dreadful coming.

If it takes devastation
to wake us up
you did it.

Immortal
yet mortal beings
are we.

GOD'S BODY

If you asked me:
Does God have a body
I would say "yes"
and it's living in me now.

Walking down the street
it could be anything
from a he to a she
to an it.

Dressed
in civilian clothes
sometimes we appear
as strangers
to one another
and yet,
each of us
is a cathedral
whose bell tolls
to make itself known.

Living in an adult world
we need to stop and say:
"I'm not a baby
but if you could picture
God's face on my face
peeking out at you
the way a newborn does
you will have touched
something beautiful."

A NEW SENSE OF BELONGING

What I want is real life
not the fake side of me
showing up on the dance floor.

Fitting in
is something
I've always been good at
but today I'm in a theatre
watching a movie
of my true self.

Excruciating in its truth
the film reminds me
no one
can put a dagger
through my heart
the way I can.

I come out of the theatre
no longer pretending
to be something I am not.

Wearing a new pair of shoes
I fit into them nicely
and go walking
down the street
as if the whole world
belongs to me
and this time
I know it does.

SING YOUR OWN SONG

When the song
of a bird
is pristine pure
you get drawn into it.

Only later
the secret
gets revealed.

It's the story
of the ecstasy
of the featherless one.

Going in search
of her own beauty
her twisted beak
gets pushed inward.

Deep down
deeper than deep
she hears
the haunting sound
of the Mother within.

This time
she knows genius
when she hears it
and nobody
can sing her Song
the way she can.

INSTINCTUAL LEARNING

Blind eyes
don't see danger
until they're standing
in the pitfall of it.

Anguishing
though it is
the instinctual part
of you
becomes fully alive.

You think
you feel
you sense
you know.

This time
when peril strikes
you don't go
pussyfooting
around it.

You just say it as it is:
There's a flame
in my skirt
with fire in it.

Wanting your own safety
the shut door opens
and you go walking through.

AUTHENTIC FRIENDSHIP

Sometimes
I see your beauty
and revel in it
until the dark side
of your face
slams into mine.

As destructive
as your curt words are
my aiming to please
is no less different.

Authentic friendship
can no longer
waffle around
with falsity in it.

Truth
must cut through
like a sword.

If the agreement
is mutual
I'll chisel away
the stone
in my heart
and return it
to you
in the form
of a pearl.

FREEDOM OF A LIONESS

Be careful
how you tread.

Too many eruptions
on the inside
can damage
your sense
of well-being.

Pretending
not to be ruffled up
when you are
can stir up
a volcano in you.

You're in training now
so tame yourself down
and let the truth
be made known.

A lion
locked up
in a cage
is what the wild side
of you
looks like.

Come out
from hiding
and you will be free.

CLEAN SLATE OF GOD

Paradoxical souls
we come stomping
out of the dark side
of ourselves
into the light.

Complexity
is what
we're made of.

Wired up wrongly
entanglement
is the knot
tying us down.

Losing our zest
negativity
pulls us
backward
into a slump.

Reversing the energy
soul
is the springboard
upward.

The clean slate
of God
we want our name
written on.

WHITE RABBIT

I'm not a wolf
but wrong love
makes me feel
like one.

I want to devour
the one
who hurt me
but I cannot.

I suppose
I could bargain
with you
but my body
is not for sale.

And even if
I chose
to kill you
my wounded flesh
would not let me.

I am soft
on the inside.

My colour
is white
and the soul
of a tamed rabbit
lives in me.

ETERNAL SOUL

Should the elements
of wind and water
sea and sky
turn against me
I would still flourish.

Nothing
is stationary
anymore
not even
the old part
of my stiffened body
growing young again.

Stepping into
the Mystery of
I know not what
everything
is moving
the darkness
out of me.

Tangible
as the breath
I breathe
yet purer
sweeter still
is the Energy
I am
cocooning in.

NEW BIBLE

Squashed down
like a weed
with a cyclamen
blooming in me
is the new way
I will present myself
to the world.

Never again
shall I succumb
to the harsh treatment
of a bulldozer
driving through me.

I shall carry
my own Bible
with me
and the word LOVE
shall be printed
on every page of it.

Even people
who put an X
beside my name
I will not hold
a grudge
against them.

I am too tall
for that.

SILENT MYSTERIOUS ONE

Fragility
like a slit
in the skin
I can feel
the pang of it
go into me now.

Yes, my Love,
before I found you
I lived
on the outside
of my inside self.

Now
it is different:
I'm evolving
always evolving
yet standing still.

And you are there
always there
like a fog horn
in the night.

It is the quiet
eerie sound
of your Being
in my being
that I have fallen
in love with.

FLARING YOUR TRUE COLOURS

A peachick
pulled down
into a graveyard:
That's what gravity
did to me.

Distressing as it is
and featherless too
I can't go on
playing the game of
"superficial is lovely"
when it isn't.

Without pretense
I need
to be myself
my whole self
my lovely self.

I need to emerge
differently
to come out
wearing
a more colourful
outfit.

I need to flare my tail
the way a peacock
does.

BIGGER BRIGHTER UNIVERSE

Losing sight of myself
I sometimes think
I'm a crooked line
on a straight page.

Forgetting who I am
I travel
in small circles
far away
from the bigger one
in whose image
I am made.

Incomplete
without the Other
I bleed for
I know not what.

Diminishment
sets in
gnaws me up
like a tooth
on the inside.

Flung open
wide open
my small self
gets plunged
into something big.

TRUE FACE OF LOVE

Captivating me
as you do
I cannot say
what it is
about your soul
that lures me
inward.

I just know
your deep
dark eyes
coming toward me
are the lens
through which
I see.

There's something
in you
like a laser
sharp
lovely
pure.

If love
can pierce me open
that way
then you
have done it
to me.

LET LOVE
GO PULSING THROUGH

Put God in a box
and the corners of it
will explode over you.

Rip the cardboard
open
and expansion
will begin.

It's an alive God
not a dead one
you're working with.

It's in the DNA
of your
soul's body
to know
to love
to feel
so why not
proclaim it and say:
God is as near to me
as my thumb is
to my hand.

Now place your fingers
over your heart
and let God's Love
go pulsing through.

WOLF-LAMB

Not knowing yourself
an innocent, sweet smile
can be as dangerous as that.

Take, for example,
the pure lamb, the white lamb
who doesn't smell danger
when she sees it.

Meek, mild and calm
she steps into her own mud
and gets covered in it.

Lamely
picking herself up
she sees how a lamb
lying in a wolf bed
can devour her.

Irrational and turbulent
she makes her way out
into the open air
breathes it in
and wraps herself up
in a redeemable package.

If you meet her
this time you will know her
wolf-lamb
strong, bold, resilient.

VOICE INSIDE THE HUSH

Divine words
flowing through me
like a soft current
no more stammering now.

Just eloquence of thought
from an interior Being
divinely orchestrated
for this moment in time.

For the bruised heart
no more straining to be heard
just compliance.

No more bloodshed
just an open heart
singing joyously
over a new found Song
remotely heard.

Listen closely
and you will hear her
swaying
in the branches
of a tree.

She's the soft wind
rippling through you
the hush
before the sound.

A TIME TO INDULGE

Like a magnet
attracting
the good and the bad
I've come to know myself
this way.

The sweet side of me
does not like dirt
and yet,
I have accumulated it.

Older now
and dragging
a garbage can
behind me
I must let go
of what is in it.

Tossing out
the negativity
I'm like a springboard
popping up
where you least expect.

Landing
with my two feet
on the ground
I'm at home now
with myself
and indulging in it.

FACE IN THE MIRROR

Living in a crushed-out world
each of us
is an icon for the other.

Some of us
more shabby than others
but each of us
showing up
with the broken bits
of something beautiful.

A crystal, perhaps,
shining through a stone
or a diamond
lying in the sand.

Whoever we are
whoever we be
each of us
is a reflection
of the other.

Each of us
an unfinished mosaic
hanging on the wall
of our troubled world.

Each of us
a face in a mirror
longing to be seen.

HERMIT SOUL

Emerging
from the quiet
I shall always
return there
for my solace.

Serenity
is the home
I live in
and yet
like choppy waters
I've known
that kind
of turbulence.

Fully in the world
yet set apart
a loner am I
who gets called
out of herself
to be
with others.

A hermit soul
needing my quiet
yet ready
to give my all.

BIRTHING OF THE WHITE ROSE

Coming out of the shadows
I am a woman in labour
giving birth to myself.

Relishing who I am
I bleed
with my own blood in it.

I sing, I dance, I hum
I say to myself:
White rose
splattered in red
I am in love
with the thorny part of you.

Wherever you hurt
I hurt too.

Be alive now
be well
sit inside
your own skin
the way the green moss
sits inside hers.

Be kind, be soft
be lovely
relish all
that is good
within you.

BEAUTY OF A BURGUNDY TULIP

Unless you knock down
the cement wall
of depression
you will end up
going nowhere in it.

So listen
to the burgundy tulip
of your alive self
not your dead self say:

"Your life
is what matters
so move on with it
become
your own
best gardener.

Plant
your bulb-like bulbs
water them
nurture them
watch them grow.

It's your beauty
not someone else's
you must learn
to cultivate."

HOW THE WOUND
GETS HEALED

If you want to leap high
look at a wounded child
and see
how she does it.

Then picture this:
a girl in a woman
returning
to her former self.

Picking up
the broken pieces
of the lost girl in her
she says:

"There's a hole
in my heart
so big
that even
when I want love
I run far from it."

Sobbing the hurt
out of her
she's the brave girl
in a woman
who knows
how to do it.

SOUL CLEANSING

Be honest
about the muck
in your soul
and ask yourself:
What
does the hollow shriek
of the rigid one
coming alive
look like?

Is it soft
warm
and cozy
like your first love
or is it strong
pure
and clean
from having
the dregs
of a sewer
pumped out
of you?

If you want
beauty
true beauty
own your truth
and let the filth
fly free.

FREEDOM TO BE ME

I want to leap
like a deer
run
like a fox
but inhibition
has held me back
for too long now.

Pinned down
by a snag
in my heart
I must stop
trying to be
something
I am not.

I must hang low
hang loose
like a leaf
falling
from a tree.

Then shaking
myself free
I shall rejoice
and be glad
in it.

PAINTED FACE ON A CANVAS

You look at me
and say:
two eyes, a mouth and a nose
but there's more to me
than that.

Dismissing me the way you do
is like running a rake
through my fingers.

Disagreeable as it is
I'll be painting my own portrait
from now on.

It may not be
an Emily Carr
or a Vincent Van Gogh
but I do know
a good portrait
when I see it.

Highlighting one's face
it could be the snag
or warp in the canvas
that brings it to life.

Painting your own face
nobody else
but you
can do it.

WHITE DOVES
IN A DARKENED WORLD

On a dark night
you might say
she was a good omen
in a black sky
turned luminous.

Befriending others
she was like a weather vane
who knew uproar
when she saw it.

She was not a doctor
of the sky
but on a bleak day
people would come
for a glimmer
of her light.

Catching on
to her goodness
the white doves
multiplied
and grew large
in number.

When permitted
they would fly
over a war zone
and make it better.

THE SIMPLER BETTER LIFE

Ripped open
by the tornado of life
she would never again
return
to that kind of devastation.

Like a good wholesome recipe
the ingredients of her life
would change
shift, alter.

Hardship
no more than a smudge
on the paper
would lessen.

Erasing past hurts
there would be clarity
without discolouration.

Her life
would become simpler
one sentence
with a period
at the end of it.

Succinctly put
living her life this way
she would go on
being happy in it.

THE DIVINE KISS
IMPRINTED ON YOUR FOREHEAD

To the pierced One
show your face
and show it now.

Hide behind no one
the wound
that is yours.

Stand tall
taller
than you ever have.

Say to God:
Take me by the hand
raise me high
higher still.

Lead me
guide me
kiss me
on the forehead
imprint your name
upon me.

On this holy day
Love
unlike any other
eternal, forever
penetrate me now.

TRANSFORMATIVE BROOK

Ashes
we all have them:
the hurts, the pains
the unfinished part
of our lives
but why dwell there
when the breeze
of a new current
comes blowing through?

Move forward
and see it
for yourselves
the blue brook
on the other side
of the pond.

Sometimes
that's all it takes
the soft lapping
of a stream
to makes ourselves
feel better.

Sitting
in the smoothest
part of our being
is not this
the luxury we long for?

CALL OF THE HEALER

Here comes the pure one
the spotless one
but even she
has streaks of grey
running through her.

Imperfect as she is
she knows Love
when she sees it.

Unnoticed by others
she says little
but the beauty
on the tip of her tongue
says it all.

Full of goodness
she comes
not like wild fire
to burn down
but to build up.

With salve on her hands
she comes
not to harm but to heal.

And to the weary
and lame of heart
she anoints their head
with oil.

HOME OF SERENITY

Living
in a cluttered-up mind
it's time you went
on a cleaning spree.

Whatever
the disruption is
take a broom to it.

Sweep yourself out
and make room
for the new
to come in.

Begin again
and tell worry
there's no place
in your kitchen
for her.

Put a geranium
in your window
and watch
its beauty grow.

At night
step into bed
and let serenity
tuck you in.

MYSTERIOUS VOICE
OF THE SPIRIT WITHIN

In the noise of life
I sit quietly
on the periphery of it.

An enigma
to myself and others
Mystery
is the realm
in which I travel.

Without
any certainty
wherever I go
She goes
with me.

You could say
it's a nothing
nowhere place
where the nomads
in exile go.

Empty
yet full,
in our
unknowingness
there is an unseen Force
by which
we do get led.

THE LOST SHALL BE FOUND

A small child
lost in the woods of life
the hunt for God
began early.

Thirsty for
she knew not what
she was a girl child
standing in a dry well
looking for a drink
when there was none.

Following a zigzag route
she went in search
of something beautiful
something
she could never quite
put her finger on.

An oasis of sorts
she knew existed
somewhere, somehow.

Momentarily
disappearing into herself
she lost sight of who she was.

All the while
hidden under the veil
God was looking at her.

NEW ROBE
TO DRESS IN

Cutting me deeply
your sharp tongue
has a razor in it.

Thorough as the wound is
I cannot hurt
or harm another
and yet,
your meanness
is enough to make me do it.

Like a slit in the skin
I can feel
the pang of it
go into me now.

Years later
I feel something
softening in me.

Something smooth
like velvet
against my skin.

Something flowing
in the wind
so gentle
I get to dress myself
in it.

OBLIVION'S GIFT

Oblivion
is the name of a woman
who knows herself well.

Burnt down to a crisp
she comes leaping
out of the dark
her torn skin
camouflaging
nothing.

Stripped to the bone
there's no shame
in her.

Goodness,
she says,
is the stab
in a punctured heart
that makes you well again.

Well-versed in life
she shows up now
with the sweep
of a smile
that could cradle anyone.

Holding on to nothing
yet loving everyone
Oblivion is her name.

THE PUSH OF GOD

Past the place
called stuck
the new
the never before
is what I'm moving into.

Limitless in its outreach
I've known
the breath of God
to move me forward
in this way.

I've seen it in others too
a new sprig
of something vital
growing in us.

Even
in the bleakest part
of our world
the God energy
can lift a mountain
when we're trying
to climb a hill.

Whatever is happening
the universe
is on its journey too
and won't be pulling back
when it's time to go ahead.

A MORE PERFECT DESTINATION

Truth comes
like a hiccup
in the night.

It wakens you from sleep
and says:
Stand still in your sterility
and you will die
move on
and you will live.

Pick up your bed now
and go
where the unfamiliar go.

Do not track
your destination
ahead of time.

Just go
believing in yourself
and know:
A dark trail
of seemingly nowhere good
will inevitably
lead you
to somewhere better.

Just go
and you will be led.

EXPOSURE

The sick crowd
dislikes
a naked soul
running down the street,
pushes you
into the background,
wants you
to put clothes on
when you can't.

Hiding disruption
only makes it worse.

Try chiselling
the mouth shut
and it will open
wider still.

Stripped down to nothing
it's the story of Jesus
re-iterated in our time.

Nobody
likes exposure
and yet,
it's rampantly going on.

Look around you and see:
The lie
can no longer be hidden.

SCARLET SUNSET IN THE SKY

Stamped on
trodden over
I am the unhealthy seed
the withered-up one
sitting naked
in your garden.

On my first death
pretending
to be a blackberry
juicy on the vine
there was nothing
edible in me
just a hard pellet of pip.

Ploughed under
by the harsh rake
of a Gardener
I got to touch
taste
feel and see
what crumpled-up
looks like.

Then came
the sweet side of me
the mellow fruit
and like a sky
streaked in red
I went running toward it.

DRUMMER
DRUM YOUR DRUM

A window
smashed in
on itself
is what cut me open
and made me
into the free agent
I am today.

No longer
sheltering myself
from the truth
I say it as it is:
Wrung out
is when the new
comes in.

Removed
from anything scientific
I'm sitting in a laboratory
of my own making.

Hearing myself sing
I'm not sure
what this music is.

I just know
it's the tap, tapping-tap
of the awakening
of a Drummer in me.

SOUL BATH

A piece
of wrecked furniture
lying on the ground
is my wayward self
leaving the old home
for the new.

Looking backwards
I'm the dream girl
waking up
to the mud
under my feet.

Agitation
a thistle
in my toe
pushes me forward
to something better.

Something bigger
brighter
fresher
cleaner.

Kicking the dirt
off my feet
I am the wayward one
having my soul
washed clean.

A MODERN DAY MARY

Unnoticed perhaps
I could be a modern-day Mary
standing in a marketplace
announcing the good news.

If you think
I'm dreaming this up
I'm not.

Have a look around
and if you see a fierce figure
gentle as a lamb
you will know
it is I who am coming.

Put me behind
closed doors
and I
the shackled one
will move through them.

Having seen God's face
in your face
in my face
in everyone's face
nothing
can stop my coming.

You may not know me yet
but I am coming.

NEW LIFE IN GOD

In my new life
I do not want something small
when enormous is being offered.

Already
in the underground world
I can feel and sense
the rumbling
of something bigger, better
more than.

Something rising
like leaven
in the dough.

Something sweet
and palatable
softer
than anything I've known.

Something warm
and holy
so holy
you can touch it
before it comes.

A kind God
fashioned
to take hold of us
in our time.

A TORCH ON THE TONGUE

Loving silence
Whisper came into our world
with an innate sense
of knowing who she was.

Loving her own company
she quickly learned
not everyone loved hers.

Never abrupt or noisy
but always feeling less than
Whisper had a way
of choking her words
down to nothing.

Unable
to lash out at others
she swallowed their spit
like phlegm
then made it into gold.

Refinement was never easy
but with Whisper
the impossible
became possible.

Speaking out for herself
you might say
a torch on the tongue
is what did it for her.

SOUL RETRIEVAL

I would never betray myself
but peeling an onion
that makes you weep
almost did it to me.

Sitting
with a small knife
in the kitchen
I felt blood
on the blade of it
go through me.

Intelligent
but ignorant of burn-out
I knew now
loving lavishly
perhaps too lavishly
had done this to me.

Nothing of significance remained
just a skeleton of my former self
and a skinny one at that.

Wrapping my arms around her
I picked up the last dregs
of something beautiful.

No one applauded me
but something genuine
in my soul did.

UNIVERSAL GOD

Ears, eyes, nose and mouth
I wake up
pregnant
in the morning
but not with a baby.

Humming my own hum
I have nothing
to hide.

My mouth
is full of Song
daylight Song.

What slips in
through my lips
is a bigger God
than the small one
I grew up with.

Sometimes She sits
cross-legged on my floor
then turns herself
into a He
when I'm not looking.

She is universal God
loving everyone
into being
and I am pregnant
with her.

OPEN AIR LIVING

Unnoticed
but anemic on the inside
I kept my secret hidden.

You may not be interested
in my history
but if you are
the vital statistics are there
should you want to read them.

Born into a royal family
I was the sunny upside girl
who went about
doing good.

My outside face
shone like the sun
but inside
something was nibbling away
at my skin.

Something dark and dreary
like a bomb
wanting to blast
its last bit of confinement
out of me.

Without diminishing myself
ever again
I went soaring into the open air.

RIGOROUS JOURNEY

Wanting purity of heart
this is what I came upon:
a solid mass of dirt.

All I can say is:
Angel of God
be careful
what you ask for
lest it destroy you
in the making.

Ripped open
by a tornado
disorderly as it is
you're climbing
through it
now.

It's the
inside journey
of a stripped down
soul
transparent
and lovely
to behold.

There's no turning back
so be diligent
get on with the work
that is yours.

DANCE THE DANCE YOU CAME FOR

Bare-boned one
if you want the muddy truth
here it is:
That knot tied up in a rope
is you.

Yes, dear one,
the jailed-in part of you
is where the criminal lives
but you're not a criminal.

Your soul is sacred
so sacred
that you need
to take
a scrub cloth
to it.

There's nothing
poisonous
in you
that can't be healed.

Love yourself
the way
God loves you.

Now dance
the dance you came for
and wrap yourself up in it.

GOD'S LOVE IS FOR REAL

Brain fog
wants to do well in life
but wanders around
in a desert
of her own making.

Sitting
in a tortured mind
of busy, busy, busy
she's a degreed person
who went about it
in the wrong way.

And yet,
tripping over
her own clutter
she came to know
a wrong path
can turn out being right.

Grabbing on
to the marred part
of her soul
she said:
Taste love
really taste it
and you won't
be saying
God is a hoax
this time.

MAKE GOD SHINE

Sitting
with God
in limbo
I get shoved
out of my home
early
out of a place
called somewhere
into nowhere.

Craving to be loved
always craving
I jump onto
the wagon of life.

Bumping into others
I taste
the frenzy of it.

You teach me
I teach you
it's all about the irritant
of being human.

And then there's God
dressed up
in each one of us
telling us
to honour one another.

LOVE IS THE DOORWAY THROUGH

Wounded
by something too deep
to put a finger on
shut me down early.

Stuck me into a pinhole
called shyness
where I felt the pinch of it
go rushing through.

Losing my identity
I went about looking for it
in the wrong way.

Then you came
with the soft gaze
of something beautiful
but I shut you out
before you could come in.

Years later
how you got through
my locked-in door
is beyond me.

Perhaps
only a shattered heart
can say for sure
what makes the wall
come down.

BUOYANT ONE

Knowing my own worth
I am more
than the clogged-up drain
in your kitchen
much more.

Even though
my soul drinks in
a faucet of clean water
I've felt
what the push of death
can do.

Felt it
for being scolded
for being who I am.

Felt it
for being number zero
when I wanted number one.

Felt it
like a tight harness
squeezing the goodness
out of me.

And yet,
climbing out of my casket
I am more buoyant
than had I never gone in.

LET LOVE BE YOUR BONFIRE

Rusting away
inside the cast of your body
you need something
bigger than gravity
to pull you up and out
of the small world
you've been living in.

Something
with big wings
wings bigger than you are.

Beyond the day
beyond the night
you need to feel
the push and shove of it
the soaring
of all soaring.

The blossoming
of your whole self
your full self.

Give it all the energy
you've got
and it will burn brightly.

Fuelled by Love and only Love
it's the one and only Fire
worth fighting for.

THE GOOD QUEEN

Falsity
gets dressed up
like a queen
and goes nowhere in it.

Tasteless
as the outside frills are
Queenie is hungry
on the inside.

Desperate for food
she feeds herself
the wrong way.

Licking her sores
Queenie
becomes a leper
and a Samaritan
takes her in.

No longer ignored
Queenie feels
what the kiss
of a lifetime can do.

From now on
Queenie is Queenie
and everywhere she goes
it's always
about doing good.

AUTHENTICALLY YOURS

A life is not a life
until you get gouged out
by it.

Don't pretty it up
with silk lining
when there's a tear
running through.

Just know:
People are people
and even a perfect garment
can show up
with sackcloth in it.

In a flustered world
we're like fingers in a glove
each of us pointing
in a different direction.

Complexity
is the garb we wear
so choose only
the clothes on the rack
that fit.

Dress yourself accordingly
and come out of the cupboard
wearing the outfit
authentically you.

GOD PRESENCE

Like a vortex
swirling down
to a place
called nothing
I've felt
the clean sweep
of it
go through me now.

Something pure
and pristine
like a splash
of the unknown.

An alive stillness
beyond
imagining.

The stillness
of a clear lake
on a summer day
without
one ripple in it.

A wordless something
where I become
everything in it
God today
tomorrow
and forever.

NEW FACE OF THE GOD LOVE

Victorious in life
you came
out of the cupboard
apologizing to no one.

"It's all about the secret,"
you said:
"Stop keeping it hidden."

In you, in me
God comes
like an infant
in a buggy
and no one
can stop
the fusion of it.

Pushing up the ground
of our being
God says:
"We are new souls
living in ancient bodies
we are the risen
rising ones.

Strike a match to us
and watch the flame
of Love
go blazing through."

EXPANDING UNIVERSE

Imagine yourself
a thousand times bigger
then move into
what you are becoming.

Whatever you feel
don't be jarred-in by it.

Just know:
bursting the closed lid open
is the power of God
working in you.

Now picture the universe
sitting at your desk
with a blunt pencil
sharpening itself up
to write the story of the many.

Centuries have come and gone
and you are in this one.
Others will come after you
like fire
to blaze a path
only they can tread.

As for the universe:
It will go on expanding outward
and there will be no end
to the Love found in it...

PULSE BEAT
OF THE NEW ENERGY

Peeling away
the dark side
of myself
I am future-oriented.

Sitting encased
within my body
is like driving a vehicle
I have never driven
before.

It's like squeezing the air
out of an old tire
I no longer
get diminished by.

With my soul intact
I'm travelling
in new zones
that can no longer
be calculated.

For miles around
I can see
the vastness of it.

Invigorated by God
any stale energy
is leaving me now.

SHOE POLISHER

Unpolished shoes
smothered in dust
get to know yourself
the way God
knows you.

Then say to yourself:
Liberated
from the crushed-out
heel
in my shoe
I am walking
more freely now.

Other displaced souls
are out there
on the rugged road
walking with me.

Our slogan is this:
Doomed to failure
no more
never again
is the God we worship.

Abounding in love
She is universal God:
Sister, Brother, Mother
Father of us all.

GREENER DAYS

Living
in the parched-out part
of a dry well
it's time to move on
to something greener.

As for the lump
in your throat,
the clogged-up part
of you
will speak again.

Fluidity will flow
and like a swampland
in the desert
you will drink it in.

Asleep or awake
aridity
will drive you
to the river's edge.

Drooling for moisture
your long tongue
will sip it in.

Even a drizzle of God
will quench
the thirst
you long for.

MOTHER LOVE
BIRTHING HER TRUE SELF

A nightmare
walking down the street
pretending
to be something she wasn't.

Loving everyone but herself
there was something
ferocious in her.

Something
like a stab in the chest
that needed her attention.

Something
like the killer instinct
of an animal
wanting to protect her.

Then came the hand
of recognition
clothing her fingers
with the flesh
of something warm
and beautiful.

It was the wound
of the Mother in her
and she gave birth
to herself.

SPIRIT LOVER

Overtly jubilant
you could be drowning
in a pool of sorrow
and still
no one would see you.

Humanly speaking
you could be trapped
in your own worst trap.

And yet,
falling in love with Spirit,
nothing passes through her
unnoticed.

Not even you
anxious one
tangled up in a string
of your own making.

And should your life
turn into a knot
there is nothing
She cannot undo.

And even
should you lose sight
of yourself
She will never
lose sight of you.

VOICE OF FREEDOM

Crying out for something
Whimper is a dog
who likes being held.

With dark eyes
deep and penetrating
she has a voice
shriller than yours.

A bark
louder than any lethargy
holding you in.

She's no different
than you are:
Put her on a leash
and she will run
wild, free.

Licking your fingers
she will tell you:
If you puncture anything
don't let it be
your heart, your body,
your mind, your soul.

Above all
be free:
Bark your bark
and let your need
be known.

SUCCULENT WINE

Like a berry
ripening on the vine
too forceful an energy
can squash you down
before you come to be.

As a youngster
in the vineyard
not everyone knew this
but I did.

Slow to grow
and shoved aside
it took many seasons
before the thorny part of me
could soften in the summer sun.

Years later
in the far-off fields
I could sense a widening
of something beautiful.

A sweet wine
more succulent
than anything
the vineyard had known.

And this time
all of us in it
ripening together.

TO THE DIVINE FEMININE

The details
of my life
are this:
Even
when I want love
hiding the gash
in my heart
is what
I am addicted to.

Years later
I prick open
the hard lump
and give birth
to something
beautiful.

I unleash myself
to the world
and thank God
in a way
I have never
thanked her
before.

No longer confined
to my small self
I have grown
into something
big.

GROWTH
OF THE YELLOW ROSE

Climbing up
and over
the hard-wired
picket fence
despair
is what made
you do it.

If the yellow rose
of hope
can do that
to you
then anything
is worth fighting for.

Your life
is what matters
so move on with it.

Honour yourself
pick up the dregs
of your soul.

Even a smashed dream
on the outside
can turn luscious
within.

GOD'S LOVE
THE ACHE WE LONG FOR

Stripped down to nothing
Dignity came out of her skin
more dignified
than had she never gone in.

"It's the enflamed part of my soul,"
she said,
"the ripped off part of my skin
that knows I am who I am."

Burnt at the stake, you might say:
She's a modern-day Joan of Arc
but she knows she's not that.

Then maybe Jesus of Nazareth
come back to life as a woman
but she knows she's not that either,
never has been, never will be.

And, yet,
try desecrating God's name
and she'll put up a placard
called "Love"
every time you do it.

In God, for God,
she will say:
"Love is the ache
we all long for."

WHEN HEAVEN CAME DOWN TO VISIT US

all the letters of the alphabet were rearranged
and people liked the new way better than the old.

The man-made rigid structure of God
fell apart at the seams
and everyone came out wearing new clothes
in a world that had grown to no longer despise itself.

The trumpets blew loud and clear
for the day had come
for the new world
to wrap its arms around everyone
and we all rose up more loveable
than we ever had been.

Even the sky
took on a new shade of green
and people loved what they saw.

This time the world shook us open
without any fear in it.
The sour look on grumpy faces
carried a new smile in them
more welcoming
than anything anyone had seen before.

Flexibility
ran through the blood of our veins
and we loved ourselves
into this new way of being.

SELECTED POEMS

RISK - 1975

SOJOURNER, KNOW YOURSELF - 1993

MOVING ON - 1997

WIND DAUGHTER - 1998

DANCE OF THE MYSTIC HEALER - 2001

FACE OF A GYPSY - 2007

EXPOSED - 2018

POEMS FROM *RISK* - 1975

The King's Men
Anglican, Roman Catholic and United Church Laymen's Guild

"The King's Men are discovering an increasing interest in ecumenical sharing of one's faith. They are excited by the large number of persons who are seeking the implication of their faith for daily living, and who are willing, indeed eager, to express their faith more realistically.

The King's Men commend Sister Eileen for her ability to capture the prevalent signs of God's creative spirit at work in our midst; to replace, in her poems, the doom and gloom of our cynical times with a message of hope and promise.

It is an honour and a privilege for the King's Men to be associated with Sister Eileen Curteis in the publication of this book, the contents of which reveal that faith, hope, love and peace remain the keystones of gracious and abundant living in any age."

SELF PORTRAIT

Eileen
solo singer
backwoods girl
extend to us
a trail
of your long root,
show us the tree
from which you were made.

Conceal not
the branch
of your hanging,
the rope
whose shreds
you live by.

Be for us
a sign
of delivery,
a Stream
running through
the city
of our concerns.

I KNOW HE IS CALLING

When He calls a second time
hasten to listen
and if it is you
He is beckoning
let not your face
be hidden
but go
as wings would have you go
stretching forth your hand
your right hand
to meet Him.

And if His Voice
be in the wind
you hear
let Love
lead you.

ON THE MOUNTAIN OF GOD

I
who have soared
through unknown clouds
to meet You
shall never tire
of going through
your doors.

Having seen You
I shall know
the weight
of my own mountain
that it be never
too heavy to carry.

And my own soul
I shall raise it to You
even unto
the highest heights.

YOU WHO QUENCH MY THIRST

North
South
East
West
where can I go
that You will not find me
You
who know me
better than myself
and where will I find You
if not in the open mouth
of my parched valley?

Oh, wet landscape
in the midst
of my dry field
how long I sought you
without moisture
how long!

IN YOU I STAND

Before You came
there was so much emptiness
inside the glass cage
of my straw house.

Statues
wanting to be made
out of stone
and then,
the fear
the Chiseler
would come.

Each day I would ask myself:
Who am I
and what beauty is there
in the hand of this Carver?

Years have passed
and still
I remember
how you smoothed me away
from the pain of your tool.

Today
You are the cornerstone
on which I stand.

TRUE IDENTITY

Tell me
are you a butterfly
or a spider
and what face do you wear
yours
or the worlds?

And why
if the sky is blue
conceal yourself
in the shadows?

For centuries
people have been doing this
and saying:
Love
locked up
in a cage
is a cocoon
that flies
by night

But why conceal your beauty?

Masks
are the starvation guard-rails
that we wear.

Only you can remove them.

IN TRIBUTE TO THE LOON

To form one's own lyric
and then
to be a friend
of the loon
because it is your own song
you hear.

Is not this the beauty
of your weird destiny
the pierced loneliness
with which you fly?

And what is joy
if not the echo
of your melancholy years
the shrill cry
of the bird within you.

THE WAY MY BLOSSOMS GROW

I can remember
when it was spring
and how I devised this umbrella
for the first time
months
before the avalanche
actually came.

People
were like robins then
crowding into my trees
perching
with their feathers on me.

Only sometimes
they became crows,
ravens
or even scavengers
gluttonous
for the worms
I could not give them.

Now I wait
inside my shelter.
In the drought season
winter passes through me
like a cyclone
in the spring.

SELF KNOWLEDGE
IS BEAUTIFUL

I
who have moved
out of this fog
with you
know that nothing
is private anymore
gnats
burrs
we are all tainted
by the same thing.

So why hide
your lilies
behind thistles?
Only boys do that
and you're not a boy.

Guilt grows best
when left to ripen
on a tree.
Just look at yourself:
figs
prunes
walnuts
cabbage
cauliflower –
It takes a long time
to decipher
who you are.

A NEEDED PURGING

Say to your accusers:
Is it my carcass
that you sneer
and, if so,
why do you tear
the only defense I have?

Underneath
your hairy eyes
I do not need a mirror
to detect you.

I have seen you before
in the forest
shaped like a dagger
in the trees.

Always you follow me
with the smooth blade
of your 500 hands.

It is you
I must learn
to pass through.

COME TO THIS ORANGE VALLEY
IN THE FOOTHILLS

All you soft-spoken stallions
with your craggy hooves -
Come
from your mountain ravines -
Come
to this orange valley
in the foothills.

Oh tall, spindly ones
sing
hum
dance.

Fly
with your thistles
in the breeze.

Sleep not
on the stubble
of your childhood memory.

Carry no nettle with you
just be yourself
in the wind.

POEMS FROM
SOJOURNER KNOW YOURSELF - 1993

"Artfully written by one very close to nature, this poetic pilgrimage carries the reader through an inner journey in search of the truth within. From the timid child to the sad corn girl, the compassionate one continues her journey, defenceless through roads of freedom, anguish, hunger, and abandonment, awaiting the Strong One who would heal her. One must try to love, to become free, to discern, to learn to let go until one believes "a butterfly lives deep within." The searcher befriended by Love remains a stranger to many, but her hidden beauty sparkles beyond description and makes of her a true and joyful pilgrim, inviting the reader to experience a new dimension of inner healing."

Alma Lamoureux, ssa.

"*Sojourner, Know Yourself,* invites you to look at the amazing power of healing that lies within the human spirit. It is a book of hope that conveys the belief in the fullness of life for everyone. In my own personal journey, I was called upon to let go of all the buried wounds of my past, all those negative emotions that had prevented me from being free. After a long struggle, I came forth from this ordeal more alive, more whole, more fully human."

Eileen Curteis, ssa

PILGRIM

Some avoid the road
but why should they
when the heart
is meant to travel on.

Is not this the reason
lost one, with the darkened eyes,
why each of us
walk with the bent body
of a sojourner
setting out in one direction
then twisting our way
into another
not knowing
how devious our hearts can be?

Surely, to find the right way
is the truth of any traveller.

Crooked
though our feet may be
we set out on a path
no less perilous
than the woman
who saw beyond
the bleeding of her cut hands
the remnant of the Light
she could be!

BEGINNER'S JOURNEY

It was the beginning
of a new departure
and as much
as she needed to know herself
she could not come
to this knowledge alone
so what she disclosed was
that if satchels could speak,
hers would have said:
Don't anyone climb into the body
of the shredded one
but be there
when the waves
of this restless eddy cover her.

Be there
like a lighthouse
shining in the sea
so that the integrity
of the unseeing black one
may not go unnoticed
as with daylight
she opens her mouth full of song
to the sea.

WATER JUG

When the well dried up,
she said:
I am the thirsty one
who drank my water
at all of the wrong places.

I have wandered far
in a world
that is tasteless to me.

I eat everything
but nothing
satisfies me.

Driven by hunger
I must go, now
in search of the Water
that will quench me.

THE WEEDER'S FORK

I cannot stand
the fork
that breaks the shell
and, so,
the pain
gets inflicted on me.

Split up
into small pieces
I am the timid one
stumbling
over the whole earth.

With narrow slits
in my eyes
I cannot see
beyond the darkness
of them.

Contaminated
by impure air
I am being weeded out
of a life
that is not good
for me.

CHILD

A spear in my heart
I am the small one
longing to be big.

With shoes
enormous enough
for anyone
I am alone
in a world
I cannot walk in.

A misfit always
I find no comfort
in a cushion
with thorns in it.

Bandaging
my wounds
for healing
I trudge forward
on a journey
I believe in.

CORN GIRL

Sometimes
the abundant crop
was not there
and she would wait
with her bag open.

I am the corn girl,
she would say,
who knows it all.

Driven
by the Song I sing
I yield to no one.

Inside the pretence
of a full heart
the void
has deepened
its sadness in me.

Like a singer
without song
I grow weary
from too much hollowness.

I am too shallow
to see myself
as others see me.

FILTER MACHINE

I am the shabby one
being cut out
of a garment
I can no longer wear.

A woman in rags
I stand
with the shreds
of my life
around me.

A naked soul
purified
is the dress
my Chiseler
would have me wear.

Pressed down
by my Refiner
I am being filtered out
by the One
who loves me.

COMPASSIONATE GIRL

In her girlhood
it was the image
of a bent stick
she carried with her
an image
that would always cause her
to lean
in the way of compassion
and, even though,
it had been
a crippling experience
it would not always
be that way.

Compassion was
and would be
her teacher.

If the wind
struck her down
one day
she could just as easily
take up her position
the next.

Upright
was what the wind
was teaching her
and upright
was what it would be!

FUR COLLARS

The cry of the poor
is not over there,
she said,
it's standing
beside you.

That shallow caricature
walking toward you
with fur on it
is as hungry
as you are.

Don't disguise yourself
when she comes.

Wearing a coat
to distance ourselves
only prolongs
the agony
of the unloved.

Listen!

Can you not hear
the echo
of her hollow cry?

BIRD SWOOP

Being bound in chains
is like saying
to the menace
of the birds
surrounding you:
I am a prisoner
being held in
by my own shackles.

Without voice,
I am the silent
dumb one,
who sits on the corner
next to you.

Tragedy
is my name
but you do not
know me.

Without shoes
I, too, limp
with those
who are crippled.

Can you not
see me?

FREE SHIP

Body
you are like the ship
I house.

Coming into shore
heavily laden
I let down my mast
for no one.

Pushed over
by the mean current
of a lifetime
I sail
on the sharp gouges
of these rocky cliffs.

A sailor woman am I
with a free spirit
ocean-like in my demands
tide-bearing and free
living on the land but off it
standing firm
yet driven on
by the winds of a destiny
that never claimed
to be predictable.

Capture me, you cannot!

FOOT BASIN

Like worn out shoes
the toes of the wayward one
got stubbed out early.

Each time her disability
became obvious
she could have pinched herself
a thousand times harder.

One day her own nails
did the cutting
and she cried out -
I am the red woman
with blood on my hands.

Come, oh come,
she cried!

Without a foot basin
to wash in
love is an anguish
that needs
to be tended!

FROZEN GLANCE

Maybe you do care
but how am I to know
when one day
you smile your smile
or glance your glance
then look
right through me
as if I were not there.

At times like this
I don't know
what makes me
an ice woman
or maybe I do.

Forgive me if I say
cold eyes
never make a difference
because they do!

BREAD OF LIFE

Being famished
was one thing
but when
it was your friends
doing it to you
there was no need
for that.

After too many injuries
she would say:
Starvation
is what
the heart throbs on.

At my table
forgiveness
like the smallest morsel
of a crumb
is the bread I long for.

From now on
my food
is not to go hungry.

ROADWAY COMPANION

A homeless beggar
I come to you
up out of the gutter.

I sing sweet songs
with the birds
in the ditches.

Meeting the downcast
I am no
ordinary hobo.

Derelict
that I am
I tramp the streets
where they are
that my joy
may be full!

ROOTED TREE

Under a joyful face
there lay the blank stare
of the saddened one.

Hidden
in her clay pot
were the crushed seeds
that wanted to die
but could not.

Hers was a life
full of pain
with roots
so huge
you could not
see them.

In times of rain
she grew
beyond our imagining
into a tree
that could not
be toppled.

SMALL ONE

I am an adult woman
feeling vulnerable
as a new born.

Clasping
the small head
of the tiny child
in me
I must grow
to love her.

With twisted branches
most people think
I am as strong
as an oak
but my bark
cracks easily.

If I am to become
transparent
as a window
you see through
I must not hide
my defencelessness
any longer.

HIDDEN ABANDONMENT

Each time it was morning
and the dew would glisten
she saw
how exquisite
her beauty could be.

I am an earth woman,
she would say,
growing deep roots
under the split trunk
of a lonely tree.

At night
my love
is circular as the moon
but no one sees me.

Understand me
in my abandonment.

Behind the veil
of my broken branches
I am waiting
for the strong One
to heal me.

TRANSPLANTED

A cut down tree
and a rootless twig
died
on their way down.

She never deserved
this kind of death
and, yet,
it was the destiny
she had been
called to.

Choked out
of existence
the soil grew
like callous weeds
around her.

Under her dead body
ruby roses appeared
for the first time.

The garden
transplanted itself
and so did she!

CANDLE BEARER

Sometimes
the wax hardens
and the light you had
no longer gets reflected.

As truth
would have it
you are not
the fairy godmother
you thought you were.

This time
the beast devours you
and with
your own monster
you enter
by way
of the black door
into the shadows.

Only, then,
will you know
blindness is temporary.

Your days for burning
are never over.
The candle you were
is the candle
you are!

INDESTRUCTIBLE POCKET

The snag
in my dress,
the flaw
in my coat -
I was being dragged down
into oblivion
by them.

Each time
my garment tore
I cried out
for the Seamstress
to come
but She
was nowhere
to be found.

One day
the hole
in my pocket
grew bigger
than I could bear.

She came
and I was ready.

Love is the needle,
she said,
by which
you get stitched up.

SWEET OATS

Some vibrations
are joyful,
she said,
others are not.

When the tune
is melancholy
your body
is like a bird
without song.

In every silence,
it waits for you.

Some say,
it takes more music
for the flesh
of the wounded one
to be healed.

Others say,
like sweet oats,
it's the scar
that softens
your song.

Whatever the melody
she sings best
when the wings are free.

BOTTLE DISCERNER

To be cautious
that's what the broken bottle
like chipped glass in the mouth
had taught her.

Disheartened by her experience,
she said:
Life is a series of bottles
you drink from.
You sip out the good
until there is none.

Knowledge is like that, too.
When true wine
becomes vinegar
you learn to discern
what is best for you.

In that way
the drink
becomes delectable!

FRENZIED LIVING

If she had anything
good to say
about her life
it would be
that the only sane thing
about the insanity
of a merry-go-round
is
that sometimes
you can get off.

When you do
there is no more
of this
whirl me, whirl me,
round I go
as if in a frenzy
but rather
it's an unburdened
way of living
where like a kite
the load gets lifted.

GRASS GIRL

Each morning
the grass girl stood
in the middle of a still field.

It is here
I must find my centre,
she said.

In the distance
she could hear
the noise of the city
calling to her.

People rushing
in all directions
feet going nowhere
in a flurry
cars
bumper to bumper
at a standstill
and she being drawn
into the whirlwind
of it all.

I must answer
the needs of my people,
she said,
but never will I be anything
but the grass girl to them.

LIFE'S HARNESS

Already
the gnawing
had set in
and as much
as she wanted
to untie the knot
in her rope
she couldn't.

Like a horse
without halter
life is a harness,
she said,
I want to get out of.

Learning to let go
is like flying
with my mane
in the wind.

One day
I shall make it.

FREE FLYER

In every storm
I am the downcast one
learning to fly.

I try hard
but like stiffened wood
I cannot
flutter my wings.

Each time
I encounter stone
I know
what I am made of.

A butterfly
lives in me!

FOREST HUNT

For so many years
it was like being lost
in the huge forest
of a small girl.

Finding her way
was difficult.

In these woods
where nature
was at its best
she learned to love
the bark on every tree
as if
it were her own skin
she was wearing.

In the densest
part of the forest
she discovered how green
her home could be.

Here in this woodland
she met other persons
who were like her
and together
they sang their song
of creation.

VOICE OF INNOCENCE

Like the pure gushing
of a waterfall
I will know it
when I hear it
this voice
of innocence in me
the one
and only voice
worth making a sound for.

With unclean heart
I have gone
in search of her
from the very
beginning.

A wanderer in distress
she has led me
down a path
to where the stream
flows free.

On a clear day
you can see me
sitting with her.

BULRUSH WOMAN

When you found me
carrying a bulrush
in the meadow
I knew
from your looking at me
there was something
of a kindred spirit here.

In the solitude
of a quiet space
nothing was said
or spoken
we just eyed each other
something
like a deer
in the woods does.

From then on
we knew
we were friends.

YARN MAKER

Like an unmade sweater
longing for completion
she would have to become
her own yarn maker,
she said,
because nobody
could supply her
with what she needed.

Each winter
she would take it
upon herself
to be an innovator
of her own heat.

Fuel me from the inside,
she would say,
for I am the frigid cold one
who longs
to have her body warmed.

Years later,
after the drought season
had passed,
the yarn maker
came out of her furnace
stoking her own fires
with an energy
that could never be dissipated!

FIRE BUSH

No
you are not
a common bush
nobody
takes your zeal
from you.

It just goes
and, yet,
if you have been
in touch
with the flame
that fans itself
into a fire
if you have known Love
in this way
then you can bear
the worst
and best of anything
and know
that nobody
takes anything from you!

SUNBURST

The Voice said:
Woman,
it is not good for you
to be wrapped
in smog
any longer.

Come out of the fog
you have been in
and I
will illuminate you
like a sun
from the inside.

Pushing back
the clouds
she came forth
out of a blurred world
hard to be in.

Finding herself, now,
flooded
with the warm rays
of summer
she let
the Light come in.

MOTHERHOOD

Down by the water
the bruised reed grew
until it was her time
for nurturing.

Mother, father, sister, brother,
she said,
it doesn't matter
who we are
the mother instinct
is in all of us.

To cultivate
a garden well
we must grow our plants
without weeds
and to be food
for another
we must uproot ourselves
many times in this life.

How else,
said the neglected one,
can we stand
on fertile soil
and live?

MORNING WHEAT

Drinking the dew
of morning
I am the quiet daughter
in the flowing field
of your yellow grain.

My name
is Joy
for all seasons.

Before
even I began
my journey
I was formed
in the tough womb
of my mother.

With warm tears
welling up
like fountains
over the earth
she gave me
the birth
I am grateful for!

SEARCHER BEFRIENDED

To find her way
she was given a map
with a zigzag line
running through it.

Driven
by the wild heart
of a wolf
each maze
she went through
confused her more.

A companion
to herself
but a stranger
to many
she let in
the tamed rabbit
at the door.

White one,
she said,
I have come
to know myself
in you.

AESTHETIC BEAUTY

Such beauty
in the eyes
of this person
deeper
than the fragrance
of a rose
and more transcendent
than a sunset
by the sea.

Hers was a mystery
of brightness.

Hidden
in the deep grit
of her soul
she had travelled far
to find
how the diamond
sparkles!

RETURN JOURNEY

Oh sturdy woman
in the soothing cry
of a gentle breeze
return from your journey
with a knowledge
that will renew you.

Say
to the broken-hearted:
In my desire
to be made whole
I have been there
with you.

Called out
of the ruins
I am the fragmented one
climbing up
onto the rungs
of my ladder.

I have no home
but this one.

To ascend my Mountain,
all you who are weary,
come with me
to the breaking point!

RAINBOW PEOPLE

Deep down
in a cavern
called Love
an abandoned bird
sang her song
for the first time.

Yes, my people,
she said,
I am the crooked-winged one
who could not have flown
without you.

In a deserted nest
you found me
like a rainbow
in the sky.

It is for you
I wing my way
upward.

POEMS FROM
MOVING ON - 1997

"This cycle of compressed lyrics traces the journey of the soul through brokenness and pain to regeneration. These are tangy, surprising mini-parables for our time, moving out of silence into living speech. They display the cryptic humour and metaphoric energy of a contemporary Emily Dickinson."

Susan McCaslin, Poet and instructor at
Douglas College, New Westminster, BC,
author of *Locutions* and *Letters to William Blake.*

"Eileen Curteis is a miniaturist whose maturing skill with metaphor will startle you. *Moving On* surprises with its quirky self appraisement. The frankness of these poems makes a compelling account of spiritual/physical healing. Read it and be both jolted and charmed."

Hannah J. Main-van der Kamp
Author of *A Gift of Ruin.*

POWER WOMAN

Crumpled city
go down
into the black void
of your nothingness.

Meet her
who must die
the death that women die!

Taste her. Feel her.
Know her.
Without water
she sits on fire.

Driven
by the fierce wind
of a woman's rage
she does not howl lightly.

There is a power
in each step she takes
a power
that could make a wolf
soar like an eagle
even on the bleakest day.

Born of the Wind,
she flies
with wings
that cannot be tapered.

AUTUMN DESTINY

Frigid
as an iceberg in winter,
I know how it feels
to be the last
of the crushed leaves
in Autumn,
so strong
is this stripping
in me.

Knocked down,
pushed over
by one rude slap
of the wind
after another,
I don't give birth
to the white winged
graceful swan
easily,
but I do give birth!

WAIF GIRL

My heart
longs to know you,
Mother Earth,
but like soot
in the chimney
it's black here
where I live.

Beaten,
squashed down,
kicked like a stone,
I cannot die like this
and live.

"Nor should you,"
came the Voice
from down under.
"It is your turn
to bounce your ball
high over the earth.

Wrinkled,
dried up
prune of a thing,
you are no longer
the waif girl
in the fields
they ploughed under!"

WINDOW LIGHT

Dark room
filled with the torn face
of a bird
is death as imminent
as I think it is?

If so,
I'll not let dead roots
like black scabs
on a white flower
devour me.
I am too young for that!

Slay me with an axe
and see if I care
which way the knife goes in.
I am alive at forty!

Shut me down
like a closed door
creaking
and I will open wide
my desolate wings.
Newborn at fifty!

Destroy this sky bird
at your window
and in three days
she will live!

OPENING HIDDEN POCKETS

Wanting to speak,
the wooden throat
said to the silent tongue,
"I am too disfigured
to look at.

Odd shaped
my crippled legs
get pulled up
like a wobbly pole
from under me."

"Enough of that talk,"
said the caretaker.
"Hidden in purses
or back pockets,
that's no place
for you to be.

You're the kind of an animal
that belongs outdoors
blowing free
with your mane
in the wind!"

REDDEST, RED LEAF

Reddest, red leaf,
I pulled you
out of a dead twig
that you might live.

Not
that I would crush
your bones
anymore
than your tiny hands
have tried to do so,
not
that I would restrain
your tired feet
from covering
new ground
with the moccasins
I give you.

Not any of this.

But one thing I ask:
reddest, red leaf,
hanging looser
than the others
on your tree,
when will you let go
completely?

ROCK WOMAN

Let's be honest,
black cat
sneaking around
with slippers
soft as a kitty's fur,
that's not you at all!

You're in denial
about something.
Throwing rocks
into the basement
you got kicked
out of.

Pitching stones
at your own face
in the mirror,
that's more like it
isn't it?

Black cat, get real!

BERRY GIRL

White dress
stained
by a purple berry,
I'll not wear you
any longer,
nor will I
come into your house
lugging myself
like a suitcase
I cannot carry.

There will be
nothing heavy
in my basket
this time,
a little fruit, perhaps,
and a garment
less stiff
than the one I wore
in the Fall.

With the soft stone
of an angel,
I'll replace
the hardness in me,
and with the soul
of a flute
I'll dance
out of this old body
into the new one.

PEASANT WOMAN

Fluttering her wings
like a seagull
under the sand,
nobody
saw how hard
this peasant girl
tried to live.

Invisible,
as an unwanted child,
her sad arms
lay huddled
under her.

Cut fingers
scraped
out of a cavern,
limp body
dragged
over a chisel,
little nomad
did not die
for nothing.

Searching for Love
and finding it,
the heart
is the home
this gypsy
wandered into.

MOVING ON

One day
thrush
flew out of the ashes
with bones
delicate enough
to make you sing.

It was cinder girl
turning into
a woman.

Against
her stooped body
she could feel
the frailty
of small wings
pushing.

Loosening
her matted feathers
there was something
more here
than a face
chiselled by the wind.

You could see it
in her eyes,
a Power
stronger than steel
and in her voice
a lifetime's journey!

FARM DAUGHTER LEAVING HOME

This skeleton
has the brain of an angel.

Born
in the dark cave
of her mother
she cannot return there
nor should she.

A brave soul
with the heart of a scooter
she makes her way out the door
still faltering
with the unsteady steps
of a toddler.

In the big world
mistaken for sweet grass
or hay
stuffed under the barn
she could be any farm girl
munching
on her sadness.

Years later
I can still see her
leaving home
this skeleton
with the brain of an angel.

PRECIOUS PARCEL
THE SELF INFUSED WITH LIGHT

Not garbage
but courage
pulled out of a wastebasket
that's the way
my body knows me!

Face it
she says:
You're not
the only lonely whistle
on a freight train
dying in its tracks.

Look at yourself.
Nerves
shot down
to a pulp.
It's time pain
the irritable black fly
came out of you.

Small parcel
of my precious self
if this be death to me
then put a soul
in my light bulb
and let me live!

LONELY CLOWN TRANSFORMED

Funny little clown
that I am
turning my face
in the opposite direction
when the stones hit me.

Burying myself
as if the loneliness
of a bulldozer
ploughing me under
didn't matter.

Dying strange deaths
then turning up
in the soil
as an illiterate earthworm
you stepped on.

I'd like to come out
of this school
less of a hunchback
than when I went in.

A baker, maybe,
who gives free buns
to the needy
or a genius
who mends clothes
for the poor.

INNER CODE

Sometimes
the silent screams
of a small girl bursting
is what
you have to kiss yourself
good-bye to.

Sometimes
it's the violence
of broken dishes
in a woman's kitchen
that causes her
to rage
at the man
who slapped her.

Sometimes
it's the worn clothes
in a cramped suitcase
you get rid of
that brings you
to your senses.

Sometimes
there is no warning
the heart clangs
like a siren
and you must
love her!

ORANGE BUTTERFLY GOES LEAPING

Purple,
colour of iris,
thumping its joy
into me -
it's happening
something positive
like Spring.

Yes,
people of the earth,
I'm celebrating me
small one
with brown boots
up to my chin
coming out
of the black mud
forever and forever.

See me, now,
an orange butterfly.
Into the blue air
called sky
I go leaping.

Beyond the fence,
beyond the wall,
into the blue air
called sky
I go leaping!

WANDERER IN CAMOUFLAGE

It was January
the month of hibernation
when raccoon
went strutting over
the blind earth.

Unimportant
as grey light shining
on a dull evening,
she felt like Mrs. Nobody
going down in a balloon
that bursts its air.

Flat and ragged,
she could have been
the last piece
of anonymity there was.

Fortunately,
she bumped into snail,
who said:
Bless me,
for I have small feet
and travel slowly.

Bless me, too, said raccoon,
for I wear my mask
backwards
not to be seen by anyone
until the time comes.

TULIP, YODELLING THE NEW YEAR IN

Tulip,
at the foot of my garden,
if a hose could sponge me down
I'd turn out differently
this time.

Less private
and more open,
I'd put up a sign:
Faucet in the trees
oddities welcome!

Floating in on a barge,
I'd be a Persian cat
with big ears
the size of an elephant,
saying:
Look at me now,
clean as a tub
to bathe in.

Unharmed,
by the booing
of a crowd,
I'd stand there
with my lungs wide open
yodelling
the New Year in!

HOW THE GREEN ONE GREW

Many years ago
further back
than I can remember
I was in the world
waiting to be born
waiting, waiting.

I was hungry for food
real food,
the God food.

Nothing came of it
until the great day
of the hollow burp
when the vinegar of Jesus
passed down
through me.

Oh, how I hated the burp
but God was in the burp
and the burp was in God.
Finally, God spoke
and I listened.

Famished one, God said,
swallow your own burp
and live.
It will not eat you!
From then on
the green one grew.

BOX TURTLE REVIVES

Turtle had a voice
and a good one
but one day
she closed down
like the lid of a padlock
you couldn't open.

Inside her box, inside her shell,
racehorse had told turtle
not to go running,
running, running
in a relay never to be won
but she had not listened.

Wanting to be first
she played the game:
Hurdle me over
push me down
crack my head
and I'll wear a crown!

Years later,
collapsing
like a bed on the floor,
she saw racehorse
under the covers
and they became best friends,
world travellers,
hiking into the high zone
of the Unknown Way.

THE BOULDER WILL SET YOU FREE

Skidding,
over the jagged ice in winter,
I went on the tributary
of this misshapen river
to do my own rowing.
Rudderless, and without oars,
I thought I fell into the helm of God
steering.

Instead of that, I slid down
the wrong side of a skinny old cliff, crying —
Is that you, God,
gouging my face out of a boulder?

No, came the answer.
The gully is you falling into it.
Learn to love yourself
by loving your enemy the tiger.

Own it,
she's the dark shadow
in your troubled body —
angry bear, jealous moose,
sad monkey, guilty grizzly,
fearful chipmunk,
she's all part of the same person
called you.

Love her
as the only boulder worth holding!

BLADE OF GRASS QUIETLY ASSERTIVE

Sure
as a four-footed dog
goes yapping down the alley
it wouldn't be
my form of survival!

I suppose I could get your attention
by raising my voice
or barking loudly
but truly, I'd be happier
lying quietly on a blade of grass
content not to have
the rackety sound of a tractor
running its noise over me.

I know what you're thinking,
passive old woman
in a rickety rocker,
but that's not me at all!

I actually like being assertive
showing up in places
where the wrinkles are
and scooping the cobwebs
out of them.

And yet, there's a quieter me
who goes home
kissing the warts of another
and puts herself to bed.

WHITE LIGHT BEHIND THE FENCE

A woman waits for you.
She waits and waits.
A cold wind
from the inside
blows heavily on her.

To all appearances
she has the pained look
of a foreigner
but she is not
a foreigner.

Tight coat
veiled eyes
she could be
anybody's visitor
walking past you
and you would not miss her.

Living in a high tower,
she's the walled-in one
whose face is the fence
you cannot get through.

Longing for intimacy,
she's the white light
after the thick fog
leaves you.

DOOR OPENER

Fury, black stain on my towel
how dare you do this to me
how dare you say
my face is washed
my skin is clean
when the suds on my toes
know otherwise.

I've seen fury
grow like an iron
over my burnt clothes,
and I've said:
Wardrobes are the false garments
that we wear
the don't-touch-me categories
of our hundred thousand
different faces.

And worse that that
fury is my best friend
turning her face on me
with the pointed spike of a porcupine
distancing herself
in a game called love.

Go home, fury, and rest awhile
there are other worlds out there...
put a scorched match
under your door
and let the air come in!

A GOOD SOUL

Skirts, tangled in the wind,
this dog sniffs me
improperly,
pushes his nose
up my fanny,
and licks the salt
off my skin.

Shocking, isn't it,
the things animals do,
mimicking people
who cut you off
from the hip down
as if you had
something lacking.

Good girls
don't go public
but I'm not a good girl.
Only my soul is!

LIGHTHOUSE SHINING IN THE SEA

In burdensome weather,
you don't put out
the glimmer
of a lighthouse
shovelled
under the sea,
nor do you go
rough trod over her.

Treating her badly
she'll turn up elsewhere
a discarded candle, maybe,
with the eyes
of a night light
you cannot extinguish.

Feeling sorry for herself,
she's not the type
to be bathing her feet
over a bruised rock
when the foundation
has been taken
from under her.

In good weather
or bad,
she will shine
no matter what!

COMPASS MOVER

Compass
screwed into a wall,
I can't pretend
to know
where I'm going,
but I'm going!

Strapped down
like a suspender,
I'll pull up
my own trousers,
thank you,
and be on my way!

Small girl
with a crooked smile,
I'll be out there
blooming like a dimple
when the time comes.

If tragedy
be my teacher,
I'll pick her up
like a baby in a carriage,
cradling my own injury
if you please.

Choosing life,
I'll put joy
in the mouth of a dragon,
and tell her
she belongs to me!

THE GLORY OF BEING RAKED UNDER

Measles, grubs, scabs
come Spring
we'll all
be raked under,
little mud pies
shovelled
under the earth.

Words, phrases, speeches,
no amount of eloquence
can bring us
back to life,
not even nature
with its bugs
running
ecstatically over us.

What we need
is rapture,
delicious
as a piece of Mozart
to get us through
this day!

FIERCE LOVE

From the beginning
Love laces her boots
backwards.
She learns early
misfits like old shoes
get tramped over,
left behind.

Still,
Love remains
tied into them.

Wherever Love goes
Love dreams
of getting out
of the callous
she puts her foot into.

One day,
Love grows wings
big as eagles.

From now on Love knows
burnt green
is the colour of an old weed
choking the earth,
the colour of her first self
she wants to get rid of,
and so Love does!

STARCHED OUT
SOFT AND LUMINOUS AS THE MOON

Starched fingers,
I am the knotted one
with a soft comb
in my tangled hair,
the tight one
with the stiffened dress
all around her.

Hidden in a cluttered room
I sit quietly,
unwinding myself like a yoyo.
Nobody can loosen
my threads
the way I can.

Hard layers
peeled off
the skin of an onion,
face of rag woman
coming toward me,
my face
grown soft
and luminous
as the moon!

POEMS FROM
WIND DAUGHTER - 1998

"Eileen Curteis has an extraordinary gift for visual imagery that speaks deeply to the human experience. Her gentleness and compassion, her soaring spirit and, at times, her brokenness, all come through her poetry and strike right to the heart."

Richard Renshaw, csc,

Assistant Secretary General of the CRC.

"The poems in *Wind Daughter* will refresh your spirit. Like Blake's songs of innocence and experience, Eileen Curteis' poems of childhood and maturity create a rich banquet of both sweet and bitter offerings. Taste them, for they are nourishing, yet partake of them in small doses, for they are also potent."

Diane Tolomen, Assistant Professor of English

University of Victoria, B.C.

"Genuine feeling from intense suffering experienced by a poet frequently produces beautiful and convincing poems, as in this volume by Sister Eileen Curteis. The reader need not have met Sister Eileen to recognize her pain and her joy because they are the pains and joys of all humanity; she speaks for each of us and captures our human journey from innocence to experience, from suffering to joy, from material preoccupation to spiritual reconciliation, and from discord to harmony in God through Christ."

Dr. Frank M. Tierney, Professor of English,

University of Ottawa.

WIND DAUGHTER

She stood there, a small shred of a thing
as the wind tore into her without mercy.
"Oh Mother Wind," she cried,
"in the heart of a sobbing tree
you bring rain upon me."
"I do that," she said,
"for without this burden
how else can the torn face
of a rag doll get ripped?"

"But Mother Wind," I cried,
"I want to be real! Make me real!"
"Suffering will make you real," she said.
"Just listen to the harsh voice
of a howling wind
and know you can't always
stop the hand that hits you, not always."

"I love you, Mother Wind," I said,
"but you tug hard
at the roots of my knotted hair
and like the slit of a cold knife
going into me
it hurts where you enter."
"Yes, my child," she said.
"It hurts where I enter. Pain always hurts."

Grief knew no words and I was silent before her.
"Wind daughter," she said, "you are real.
This last ache has made you real.
Go now to the others."

SMALL'S WORLD

I

Small
is a little girl
who lived sometime
before the war was over
but for Small
the war was never over.
It was just beginning.

One day
Small told her friend:
"When war comes
do not remove these hornets
from my songbirds
in the trenches
but let me hear in them
the thunder of my own bullets.
Then teach me courage
how to die
kissing the lips of my toad."

II

Small starts out early
but in the big world
Small gets crushed easily.
Small hates death.
Small hates life.
Small hates everything.
Small is never big.
Small is always small.
Death is small
as small as Small.

III

Small goes to school.
Small hurts.
Small hides.
Small goes into a corner.
Small sees no one.
No one sees Small.
Small is small,
and death is small,
as small as Small.

IV

It's dark
in Small's world.
Everything is dark.
The food is dark.
The bed is dark.
Small fears the dark!
Small fears everything!

V

Small smiles.
Small sings.
But Small doesn't know
why she does these things.
Small you see
can see no sky,
Small you see
only wants to die.

VI

Small never grows big
but big grows small.
Small pushes her way
up the stairs
and falls less often
when she gets there.
At the top
Small changes.
Small likes to change.
Small sees things differently.

VII

In the morning
Small puts seeds
on the window.
Birds come
and she sees them.
At night
she closes the door
and it is light in her room.
People come
and she lets them in.
Small is growing big.

VIII

Small likes to be big
but Small is never too big.
Small likes people.
People like Small.
Small goes out.
Small comes in.
Small
is unafraid of Small.

JUNE DAY

In my kitchen
I stopped despairing
the day
when the dead song
of a whipped bird
left me.

It was a June day
when the wasps
flew in
at the window
and not one of them
stung me,
a June day
when the weakened bird
got lifted
and the rose
stuck out its stem
for the first time.

A day like today
where I rejoice
and give thanks
that in my kitchen
hope
rises like steam
as I burst through
yet another year!

RESTING PLACE

After the whirlwind of people,
cars, busses, city streets,
brakes jarring,
tires squealing,
horns honking,
I'd give anything
to lie down
in a field of daisies
snuggled into
the pyjamas of the earth.

Propped up
on a pillow of green moss
I'd yawn at the moon
and laugh at the sun.
I'd count stars
as they twinkled
and with the whizzing
of the wind
I'd go spinning
like a top,
into the first chimney
I came to.

I'd loosen my limbs
and dangle my hair
and call it home
just to be there.

FIRE WOMAN

Blessed be the rose
that falls once too often.
She shall see God.

Blessed be her body,
the scarecrow,
that brings forth life
from the tomb.
She shall be the mother
of many.

Blessed be her spirit.
She shall bring forth stars
from a stone
and no one
shall go hungry from her.

Blessed be the air
that floats in
at her window.
It shall hoist her up
like a sail.

Blessed be the River
that springs up like a faucet in her.
It shall gush forth like a stream.

Blessed be the woman
who warms her feet
on the coals of this Fire.
She shall be heated from within!

THE GIRL CALLED WORRY

Locked in a cupboard
hiding on a shelf
Worry is a fidgety girl
who can't do things right.

In the morning
she dresses herself
but the clothes don't fit.
Worry is slim.
Worry is fat.
Worry is never
what she wants to be.

With feet too big for her
Worry goes shopping
and the groceries tumble.
Worry trips.
Worry falls.
Worry never goes anywhere
without breaking things.

At school
Worry is the timid little goose girl
who sits at the farthest end of the room.
Worry can't think.
Worry can't talk.
Worry can't do anything.
Worry sits there wondering who Worry is.

One day Worry gets sick
and the doctors
don't know that.
Nobody can make Worry well.
Only Worry can.

Back home
Worry crawls out
of the box she was in.
Worry breathes.
Worry lives.
Worry was never meant
to worry.

CHILDHOOD REVISITED AND HEALED

I want to go back and love
the shadow of that small girl
running through
a crooked patch of the earth,
to tell her
that instead of a straight path
the road ran sideways through her.

I want her to know
that I remember the time
when it was cold out
and she didn't deserve to be there.
I loved her then,
but like a thin, shelterless tree
I was not ready
to put my arms around her.

I want to go back to that small,
loveable girl
to tell her to come in out of the rain
up out of the muddy flats
onto the dry forested land.
I want to say to her:
Little ice daughter
with the rain-pierced face
of a sun girl
I never disowned you then.
I would never disown you now.

And when the last wind shatters you
I want you to come out
of this blackened sky
wearing white.
I want you to come home to yourself
you, sun daughter of an earth woman,
you, pink bud,
climbing through the green clump
of your loveliness
you, child of a woman
I have grown to love,
I want you to come home to yourself.

DAD'S AGING SILHOUETTE

Featherless creature
gone ugly in the mirror
dad reminds me
of the girl I used to be.

Squashed down like a worm
dad always made a point
of seeing something lovely
in me.

At dinner
he would say,
scrunched up lily
in the field,
you really are beautiful.

Dad always defended me.
Even at school
when children called me
wet skunk
dripping in your poo
dad assured me
there never was
a smelly bone in my body.

He saw the good in everyone
and now,
poor dad
with heart drooped over my shoulder
is as good as he ever was.

FEAR BELLOWS

We may have skin
the colour of rainbows
but in our off season
we shut down,
the air thickens,
we thicken.

We do not like the abyss
we are leaning into
that shuddering
middle-aged woman
or man
on the black edge
of nowhere.
We do not like it.

In us,
the wild wolf bellows
fear me not
but we do fear!

BLESSED LAUGHTER

Laughter
is a yellow face
with a frown turned upward.
It never pouts at anyone.

You may go in search of her
but like the curly tail
of a pink pig
rolling down a hill
she must come freely
as the wind bursting into you
or not at all.

At any time of day
she's the white candle
that brightens up our dull world.

She puts serious things
into perspective
and like a black seal
dancing on her toes
at midnight
she makes everything
wonderful!

SHY PEOPLE'S BLOOD

You who avoid my island
why do you say I am a leper,
a scab, a sore?
Can you not see me
sitting on the far edge
of the fringe outside you?
I am not the only shy person here.
There are others like me
marred by the black mark
of your indifference.

Unlike you,
our words come clumsily,
stuck to the paper.
Sometimes we sit awkwardly
like the dry well of a parched tongue.
We say nothing.

Falling apart like a broken pencil
nobody sees our loneliness
but we are lonely.

At night, it is the same thing.
Nobody sees the thorn
in the pillow we sleep on.
We are worlds apart now,
each in our separate beds.
It is no secret
we are shyly, beautifully,
wonderfully made.
It is for you our hands bleed.

FOG LIFT

I've left you
and I'm going somewhere, now.
I'm in a car,
a steel grey one.
I'm travelling to the city
north of me.
It's an enormous, big one,
too big,
for a small person
to be here
but I am here.

Feeling
like an object misplaced
I go into the stores.
I get lost
in the furniture.
A man hands me a plastic flower
and I buy it.
I don't like plastic flowers
but I buy it from him.

Later that day
I'm on an island.
I go drifting, drifting,
I don't know why I drift
but I do drift.

Finally, the fog lifts
and I see my way through
to the other side.

I'm making headway, now,
travelling in a jet
with my specs on.

This time
I don't need anyone
to tell me counterfeit
is counterfeit.

I just know
pleasing people
or giving the man
what he wants
is like selling me
an artificial blanket
I can't sleep on.

There is nowhere
I cannot fly now!

TOUGH AS STEEL

A butterfly of sorts
she comes stomping
out of her frail, delicate wings.

Frost bitten
in winter
she grows soft petals
tough as steel.

Rains come,
winds blow,
blizzards fall,
there is nothing
she can't withstand.

Like pinched skin
or burnt grass
in a stubby field
hardship
is something
she walks through.

LITTLE LAMB GIRL

Funny little girl,
with the big dint of a lifetime
all around you,
how does it feel to be flattened?

Is it lonely there, little girl,
with heart stitched up on the wall
and face scarred,
falling hard
against the wings of your body?
Is it lonely there?

And what about the bent stick
in the stub of your mind?
Can a lame girl walk blindly with it?
Can she?

And when night falls like a cushion
do you stab it, little girl,
like a hook
or do you say,
fierce things be gentle on me?

Ah yes, little girl, little woolly girl,
with the injured twig,
when night falls like a cushion
I see you walking now
with the body of a lamb.
I see you walking.

KITE THAT SETS YOU FREE

Adam committed the first sin
then Eve,
then me!
How foolish
to think God sits there
drooling like a dog
waiting to pounce on me
every time I say an unkind word.

I don't believe
what I was told
when I was little:
"White sheep go to heaven
black sheep don't,
be good
mommy loves you,
do as teacher says,
sit up straight in the pew
it's Sunday,
and don't let God see you
chewing that wad of gum!"

Ridiculous!
And yet, here I am
a brittle bird
still trapped
in the warped wood
of my anatomy
removing the last of these nails.

In my church
there will be no more rules,
no more dogmas
just God
putting a kite
on my splintered tongue
letting me fly thorn free!

STRAIGHTENED TREE GONE RADIANT

When I learned to accept
the wart, the mole,
the obstruction on my face
only then could I say
this field is beautiful,
that ocean is lovely,
but truly
I could not have said it
without you, my friends,
who have made my whole self
loveable.

In my weakness
never once did you call me
a deformity in the rain.
Instead,
you said I was the drizzle
that brings new life
to the trees
and, so,
I shot up in your presence
as one who knew
what it meant to be straightened.

THE BIGGER BRIGHTER WINDOW

Candles look best
in dark cellars.
They are the breeding ground
of the flame
that lets you see.

For the most part
we create our own houses
without windows.
We see
only what we want to see:
rats, spiders,
elephants with long tails,
urine on the face of a mouse -
the attributes
of our own declining empire.

But why
look in the mirror
this way?
You could be different
less heavy
like a basement
pulled up
by the wisp of a string.

In the end
everything will be made easy
even death on a trolley
so wheel yourself in!

THE RETURN OF SPRING

I have never
hated anything before
but somehow
your coldness
is getting to me.

Like most good people
the moment ice
reaches me,
your ice,
I detest it
as the worst enemy
my skin
can encounter.

Still,
you have the power
to melt me.

I cannot say when
or how
this will happen
but when
it does happen
I will welcome you
as the fresh bloom
of the first one
into me!

AUTUMN'S CRUNCH

Happiness
has to be more
than a wooden doll
or a stuffed scarecrow,
more
than the flat bounce
of a coin
or the rude push
of a person,
more than a girl
calling
"hollow, hollow."

In the worst devastation
happiness
has to be picked up
like a crocus
in the spring
or a crunched-out leaf
in the fall.

It cannot exist
otherwise.

LONELY STANCE

She came into our world
something like an orchid
fragilely beautiful
but exotically different.

A stranger always
she ached to be born
in some new way
where the distance
of touch
would no longer mean
having to be destroyed
by someone
holding her.

FLUTE PLAYER

Your touch
invades me
like the dawn
and I run
with the flute
of a shepherd in me.

Oh earth, I say,
land, sea and sky,
all burdens cease
when I bear
the wonder
of you.

POEMS FROM
DANCE OF THE MYSTIC HEALER - 2001

"Sister Eileen has composed this volume of poetry to share herself in process, the process of a spiritual journey into joy and health. Only gradually did Eileen discover the wellspring of this joyous creativity in her own heart and soul. As you read these poems you, too, may glimpse the path to becoming your own true self."

Mary Brown, ssa

"*Dance Of the Mystic Healer* has Sister Eileen's trademark strengths as a poet: startling imagery, lovely repetitions, and unique comparisons. These song-verses show where Sister Eileen started as a poet over thirty years ago and point to the visionary origin of an individual voice."

Hannah J. Main-van der Kamp

"Inspired through guidance from within, Sister Eileen continues her remarkable journey towards self-realization. Her uplifting poetry of the often painful and poignant trials of life brings hope that there is a purpose after all. We have only to, in the words of Joseph Campbell, "follow our bliss" in order to find it."

Madeleine Morris

DANCE OF THE MYSTIC HEALER

My heart
Is like a spring of hope
Running down
A mountain slope

To tell a world
It's really true
The mystic dance
Belongs to you.

Sometimes you want
To skip and run
And let in laughter
Like the sun.

Sometimes your soul
Is full of pain
And then the dance
Begins again.

Sometimes your faith
Might die on route
And then your tree
Sends forth new shoot.

Sometimes the rose
Might lose its bloom
And then, the face of God
Re-grooms.

The Spirit's way
Is vast and deep
The road to God
So very steep.

HEALING IS A LETTING GO

Letting go of the shadow
Letting go of the hook
I've grown to love my story
Each chapter in my book.

Letting go of the rules
Letting go of the norm
I've become an anonymous author
Unable to conform.

I write with bold expression
The words are always true
I do not judge the contents
The way my confreres do.

The pages and the binding
Once ripped and torn apart
Have become like nagging batteries
You have to charge and then restart.

No longer in a cupboard
Where moth and dust consume
I'm going forward with my message
It's time for me to bloom.

Experience has been my teacher
Sweet ointment on the skin
The wrinkles now have vanished
And the sunshine's pouring in.

My story has expanded
Beyond the bitter weed
Like an elastic bending freely
No longer rigid in its need.

Life is one huge banquet
That a healer comes to know
Each time there is an exit
Means another letting go.

CONTENTMENT

I've moved through the puddles
And I've moved through the silt
To a new kind of soil
Where I no longer wilt.

I've known the flood of tragedy
That washes through the mind
And clears the cluttered corners out
To make a person kind.

Nothing now disturbs me
Not even worms or grubs
They all play a part
In producing healthy shrubs.

Finding out my purpose
After years of going astray
I'm building a stronger, better home
On rock that won't decay.

I'm replacing the shaky ladder
For something much more stable
And instead of fancy roses
I'm putting poppies on my table.

I'm learning to travel lightly
In a simple home-made skirt
And I've inherited a sprinkler
That children love to squirt.

I'm deleting the word called "cranky"
From the vocabulary of my mind
And I'm opening up my curtains
And pulling up my blinds.

My comfort level is very high
Like a baby sucking milk
And even were I clothed in rags
My heart would say, "It's silk!"

THE MESSIAH LIVES IN US

The leper inside me
Turned into a dove
And every time I thought of Him
I knew I was in love.

Unwrapping all my fetters
And bursting my cocoon
I felt His healing power
Morning, night and noon.

I had heard of the Messiah's journey
That happened long ago
And it gave me hope and courage
As His story was retold.

Standing on Calvary
With a butterfly in His hand
They crushed out the beauty
Of this holy Man.

They wrapped Him in linen
And shoved Him in a tomb
But now He walks in people
Like a flower in full bloom.

Opening my eyes
And shifting my lens
I recognize Him, now,
In the signs that He sends.

A waft of positive Energy
On a balmy summer day
I know it's Jesus of Nazareth
Pushing the clouds away.

His Spirit, now, lives in us
With bonfire heat
And to our broken world, He says,
"Come, picnic at my feet."

ROAD OF COMPASSION

A haphazard jigsaw
Scattered on the floor
I'm the blind woman walking
Who is healing at the core.

Squashing all my feelings
They've become like stinging bees
And the hurricane inside me
Is uprooting every tree.

No longer living in silence
With my mouth inside a sling
I'm repairing all the damage
That this kind of violence brings.

My roots are strong and gnarled
And my branches twisted in the wind
It's the prayer of an icon
That keeps growing deep within.

I'm a woman on a journey
Who's been struck by many a stick
But I've overcome the judgement
That can often make one sick.

I'm a woman who is healing
From the bitter rind she ate
And putting sugar into honey
Before it is too late.

I'm on a sacred journey
Free of human wrath
Because the shoes I walk in
Are travelling down God's path.

I've dipped into compassion
Where the mighty river flows
And the Love I've always longed for
I, now, have come to know.

WHY I MUST BE BEAUTIFUL

I took a child
By the hand
And sat with him
Upon the sand.

"One day," I said
"You'll be not small
What will you
When you grow up tall?"

I knew he did not
Really know
The query on his face
Did show.

He climbed up then
Right on my knee
And looked straight in
My eye to see.

He liked my face
It didn't hurt
I held him close
Against my shirt.

He looked at me
As if to say
I want to be like you
Some day.

INNER RISING

Rolling rocks
And shifting sand
I've often wondered
Where to stand.

My saddened feet
Have always slipped
And often have I
Lost my grip.

The ground
On which I've tried to walk
Has left me full
Of ragged shock.

Inward gullies
Ask me why
No city, town,
Or home have I?

They tell me
Not to fear this place
That one day soon
I'll win the race.

For loneliness
That digs down deep
Will cleanse my heart
And make it leap.

And when my soul
Shall strip me bare
Inner rising
Will I share.

WINTER WIND

Winter wind
Why must you blow
In regions that
I do not know?

Why must you haunt
And linger near
When well you know
How much I fear?

Why must you chap
And break my lips
And leave them here
Like paper strips?

"I do it, child,
Not for your ill
Nor for your body's
Heart to kill.

Nothing would I
For your harm
But that you lean
Upon my arm.

Your life
I long to make it free
If trusting all
You give to Me."

RADICAL TURNING

I stood on the shore
I looked out to sea
The ocean threw
Its waves at me.

I called to the mountain
I called to the sky
But only a seagull
Heard my cry.

I ran toward the rocks
Like a darting eel
So hungry was I
For want of a meal.

Around me, now,
A wind-forced gale
Had covered me
With pelting hail.

I could not see
Beyond this storm
The haunting figure
Of His form

And so I screamed
And yelled aloud
"Remove from me
This blinding cloud!

I cannot live
Inside a boulder
Without your Hand
Upon my shoulder."

And so He came
With sudden force
To turn me back
Upon my course.

WISDOM

Wisdom is something
You cannot explain
It grows in the darkness
It grows in the pain.

It withers your lips
It shrivels your bones
It walks you through deserts
Where you live all alone.

It kneels beside you
Makes fountains to flow
Speaks to your heart
That which you did not know.

It leaves just as quickly
Through the door that it came
But tread where you will
You will know it by name.

RAINBOW LIVING

I swallowed a rainbow
Out of the sky
And now I'm not
Afraid to die.

I have a garden
In my heart
And at the bottom
Rainbows start.

They raise and arch
Their coloured backs
To give me what
I sometimes lack

A heaven lovely
Like a dream
So on you rainbow
Let me lean.

Sometimes the colour
Turns to mud
When hardship hits me
With a thud.

And, yet,
No rainbow turns to dust
Unless the hand
Pulls back its trust.

Rainbows heal
In time of drought
And turn
The human heart about.

God who made
The rainbow first
Will always quench
The human thirst.

NEW VISION

Tossed about so often
By the stormy waves of the sea
I've known many a friendship
That's turned its back on me.

I've felt the waves of anger
Burn holes inside my heart
And I've tasted ugly jealousy
The dagger and the dart.

I've struggled under water
Where my ship went down at sea
It's taken many a century
To purge the darkness out of me.

It's led me to a freedom
That flows with graceful ease
Where God is my parachute
Blowing in the breeze.

I've travelled through the heavens
And I've travelled down on earth
I've named my joy ecstatic
Like a mother giving birth.

People are my teachers
In them I see God's face
Babies, infants, children
Whatever creed or race.

A cat, a dog, a monkey,
A plant, a bird, a tree,
The stars and all the universe
Are precious gifts to me.

My world view is changing
I've been stretched to greater heights
God is the pilot
And my plane is taking flight.

FOREST HOME

I've lived a forest fire
I've known its raging heat
And often have I faltered
In the midst of black defeat.

I've seen the timber crumble
I've seen it smoulder with a spark
And standing on the hillside
I've heard a lone dog bark.

I've harboured all my feelings
Like guilt and fear and rage
And now my earthly body
Must heal as I age.

My broken heart has suffered
In silent, hidden pain
But underneath the ashes
I've found it green again.

The plants are big and luscious
The trees are strong and tall
Like me, they've learned the lessons
Of winter, summer, spring and fall.

These woods where I have wandered
Are filled with sheer delight
I've grown through the darkness
And my eyes have gained new sight.

AN EAGLE WOMAN'S JOURNEY

So full my heart
Of every fear
I never thought
I'd learn to steer

But now my ship
So sure it rides
And know I how
To meet the tides.

Drowning once too often
And losing my earthly crown
I'm a woman, now, relaxing
In a boat of chocolate brown.

I'm travelling toward my Maker
Toward that secret, hidden Source
And I'm hoisting up my sail
That will keep me on true course.

There's an Eagle on my shoulder
Wanting to take flight
And I tell her that I'm ready
For the highest, highest height.

I've grown to love her feathers
Matted and sometimes torn
And in my limping body
I've been shaped and now reformed.

An eagle is an eagle
Who must soar to find her way
And, though, the black clouds blind her
She senses Light in darkest day.

Her Spirit is like cedar
It stabs you with its scent
And her journey is a high one
With wings that can't be bent.

EXOTIC FLOWERS

His real rose
I wish I were
But sordid things
Are very poor.

Their stems are heavy
Laden with grief
Their thorns stick out
From every leaf.

They suffer in silence
Without any tears
They live like this
For years and years.

The Gardener secretly
Ploughs the earth
Their petals get shaped
And ready for birth.

They turn into orchids
That look like a rose
Exotic, spectacular
But nobody knows.

They climb over trellises
They climb over gates
And arrive at a stature
Exquisitely great.

Their essence is lovely
It goes straight to the heart
Like beautiful diamonds
That set you apart.

Only an orchestra
With a fine-tuned ear
Can look at these flowers
And know what is here.

CONTEMPLATIVE HERON

Looking in the mirror
At all my defects
There's a silent heron in me
That will one day stand erect.

Travelling in circles
And caught inside a maze
I'm a contemplative heron
Who loves to sit and gaze.

Living in seclusion
Beneath an azure sky
I ponder all the quiet things
As they go passing by.

A mother with her baby
Who's singing like a thrush
Or a spider in her silken thread
Who's never in a rush.

An elegant morning peacock
Strutting toward the dawn
Or a fluffy little duckling
Who visits with a fawn.

A tiny infant chipmunk
Scurrying up a tree
Or a monk who gathers acorns
With a squirrel on his knee.

I'm a wise, observant heron
With schedules heavy as lead
But when I watch the robin
I drink from heart and not from head.

I'm like a detective dancing
Every time I find a clue
The rhythm of the universe
Lilts back and forth in me and you.

DAD'S LOVE IS A LAMP

Termites chewing
Away at the beams
Dad's house was falling
Apart at the seams.

A beautiful sunset
Infused inside our breath
My father was dying
A hero's death.

Imagine a truck
Driving through the brain
That's a picture of my father
Who never complained.

Imagine a door
That opens up with grace
Then picture all the goodness
On my father's human face.

Imagine a smile
That could make a garden grow
That's the picture of my father
Whom others came to know.

Imagine a ball
That bounces up to God
That's a picture of my father
Who walked upon this sod.

Imagine a lamp
That burns both night and day
That's a picture of dad
Who lit our earthly way.

Imagine a mountain
That is higher than the sky
It's the Spirit of my father
That will never ever die.

HEART OF ECSTASY

Inside my heart
Where others don't see
Is the Stranger
Who walked through Galilee.

I began this journey
In a body called "Small"
Where coping with life
Was a difficult haul.

My soul got orphaned early
In its quest for inner peace
The wanderer got twisted
And full of human grease.

God named me soaring sparrow
Without a place called home
And I travelled empty-handed
In this world where I roamed.

I grew to love my nothingness
In clothes that never fit
And learned to walk my journey
With a woman's graceful grit.

My soul became ecstatic
In a field of summer bliss
And my heart went dancing madly
Toward the goodness it had missed.

Like a squirrel running freely
With its fur against my skin
I saw the beauty of God's playground
Where the love comes flooding in.

My heart became a Ferris wheel
Full of human care
And the circle it created
Went spinning through the air.

COUGAR LOVE

The lamb that got eaten
As chunks of prey
Is healing herself
In her own kind of way.

No longer naive
No longer a child
There's a cougar in her
Running wild.

Chasing her tail
Getting in a flap
She falls into bed
But can't take a nap.

Stored up anger
Hidden in her bones
This cougar of hers
Is tough as stone.

She looks for God
On a beautiful float
But the long years of anger
Keep sizzling in her throat.

Filtered water
Dragging out the dirt
Cougar struggles
To let go of every hurt.

God puts fire
In the volcano of her mind
Burns out the dross
So cougar can be kind.

Cougar, now, is mellow
She struts about in truth
Wise, old animal
Converted in her youth.

MYSTIC WOMAN

People throwing
Boulders, rocks,
Raccoon is hiding
In her box.

Stop the theatre
Shut it down
Racoon is moving
Out of town.

No more acting
No more play
Racoon is moving
Far away.

Muscles tight
Locked in strain
Holding all
Her body's pain.

Raging anger
Makes her feel
Love so deep
The wounds can heal.

Honesty
Without denial
Racoon has learnt
To walk in style

Mystic woman
Full of grace
Gladness streaming
Down her face!

SPIRIT MOTHER

I asked her for music
That she course it through my veins
She left me in my prison
To stumble on my chains.

I asked her for music
To soften all my fears
She gave me empty nothingness
Shot through with bitter tears.

I called her Spirit Mother
You who know what's best
Yet living in my body
Was like failing every test.

She sent me to a school
Called "Inner Foreign Way"
I could not face my suffering
It worsened day by day.

She promised to relieve me
From this hammer driven nail
But her Son who lived before me said
I, too, would have to fail.

My future looked quite dismal
Without any joy in store
And then, like shattered sunlight
She blazed it on my floor.

I did not ask for music
Nor buds upon a tree
Yet all that had been barren
Was now green as green could be.

I called her Spirit Mother
She who danced within my soul
My music, now, was brighter
And my garden, it could grow.

FIRE TESTED

Test your freedom
Let it pang
Obstacles
In cobwebs hang.

Success is failure
Inside out
Happiness
Turned round about.

Life's a struggle
Streaks your hair
Put on boots
That you can wear.

Tramp through ditches
Plough through snow
Let the blizzards
Come and go.

Harness fire
Wind and sleet
God's love
Is in the cavern deep.

Life's a whistle
Let it blow
Harshly, gently
Watch the flow.

FREE SOUL

A ship turned over
By many a storm
I am the lamb
That has been shorn.

Life is a journey
I'm on a cruise
What direction I take
Is for me to choose.

My heart is a compass
Wild and free
Travelling inward
So I can see.

My mind can be noisy
Shrill like a horn
Leaving me restless
And sometimes torn.

My body cries out
With an ache and a scream
The pathway gets clouded
And so does my dream.

My soul is like radar
With spiritual Light
It picks up messages
On a foggy night.

The Spirit flows in me
With the force of a tap
My way gets charted
Without book or a map.

Life is a journey
I'm on a cruise
With God at the helm
I have nothing to lose.

JOYFUL PILGRIM

For years and years
I stood and stared
And all I saw
Was winter there.

Today I stand
In place the same
And know it
By another name.

Fertile soil
Green with moss
Now covers up
My hidden loss.

Ground that once
Was hard as clay
Has turned my hardship
Into play.

Tired feet
That walked the land
Are sitting, now,
In softest sand.

Thorns that once
Caused flesh to bleed
Have sprouted into
Springtime seed.

Snowdrops, crocuses,
Flowers galore
Are healing my senses
And much, much more.

Joyful pilgrim
On the move
Can't get stuck
Inside a groove.

MELODY MAKER

A lark am I
Hidden in the grass
You'll hear my music
As you pass.

The lyric tone
Of every note
Is hidden
In my tiny throat.

Sometimes my voice
Is very shy
I do not know
The reason why.

Perhaps, my feathers
Have been clipped
And in my shame
I have been stripped

Or like a bird
That pays the price
I've let myself
Turn into ice.

It's taken years
For the Fire to burn
Scalding my heart
So it can learn

That frozen feelings
Stuck in pain
Can learn to flow
And live again.

God's flute is soaring
Through my soul
Healing my life
And making me whole.

BELOVED TEACHER, YOU SET ME FREE

How happy I am
How well you teach
Every day I fly
Away from their reach.

They clip my feathers
They pull at my beak
I'm a strange little bird
Both strong and weak.

They pluck out my eyes
They tear my skin
I'm a courageous bird
Deep down within.

They scoff at my bruises
They put me in a cage
I try hard to love
But I end up in a rage.

I'm not made of plastic
And I'm not made of wood
I'm just a small, sensitive bird
Trying to be good.

They hold down my body
But I fly away free
Because my Maker
Teaches me

To soar upon
His winged arm
Free from
Any kind of harm.

Learning to love
With no reward
I fly through life
Without a sword.

SLOWING DOWN

Round and round
Everyday I'd turn
How long it's taken me
To learn

That spinning wheels
With broken spokes
Must learn to carry
Heavy yokes

That I
Who never liked to suffer
Must walk through life
Without a buffer

And now,
That I have crossed this ridge
I'm standing on
A different bridge.

Changing my patterns
And accepting my flaws
I'm learning that life
Doesn't have to have claws.

Happier, now,
In a race coming last
I'm tired of running
At a pace that's too fast.

I've taken a detour
On a road less rushed
My mind is noisy
And it wants to be hushed.

Slowing down schedules
Slowing down time
I'm a grandmother clock
With a new lovely chime.

WOMAN OF RESURRECTION

Buried alive
I might as well be
For that's the way
They treated me.

"Get into your casket
Get out of our way,"
That's what they always
Had to say.

So small was I
I did as they said
And closed they the casket
Right on my head.

I lost my power
I gave it away
My heart of stone
Became like clay.

My hardened ground
Now full of weed
Was aching for
A different seed.

My toughened voice
Was growing bold
While waiting through
This winter cold.

At last
The Potter shook my earth
And changed my graveyard
Into mirth.

Inside me, now,
A beautiful Light
The lamp of God
Shines soft and bright.

LIFE A PARADOX

Born to be free
Yet made to die
Born to laugh
And made to cry

Born to sing
Yet made to weep
Born to run
And made to creep

Touch the two
And know of life
No beauty is there
Without strife.

In me
The weather changes, too,
Thunder, lightning,
Sky of blue.

I look at life
From opposite sides
Like the ocean turning
Over its tides.

I wade through waters
In which I could drown.
I come up happy
And free as a clown.

A pessimist
Falling into the gravel
It's up to me
Which way I travel.

A smile first
And then, a frown
I'm the optimist
Turning it all around.

HOLY LOVE IS FOREVER

Deficiency marked me
Like a finger in the sand
So was it that He touched me
With the joy of His own hand.

Disguised in finest clothing
So others couldn't see
I hid my terrible nakedness
My utter poverty.

I wandered as a gypsy
With colours bright and bold
I longed for lasting happiness
That can't be bought or sold.

I wandered through the wilderness
With sackcloth on my head
And came upon the Artist
That my soul would one day wed.

He looked at me quite closely
He dabbed me with His paint
The love He showered on me
Was free of tarnish, free of taint.

His brush was, oh, so gentle
It carried not one yoke
His hand was firm and steady
And so, was every stroke.

He lifted all my burdens
And did a cartwheel in the air
His love was huge, gigantic
And filled with holy care.

I saw the heavens open
With wonder and surprise
And I knew it was forever
When I looked inside His eyes.

THE PLACE CALLED HOME

You cannot love
The sun of day
Unless the sky
Be sometimes grey.

You cannot love
The morning light
Unless you've seen
The dark of night.

You cannot know
The face of God
Unless you've walked
Upon this sod.

If all you sought
Was summer bliss
Just think
Of what your soul might miss.

So journey on
Move further still
Welcome every
Kind of hill.

The road is steep
Where you must tread
No sign of how
You shall be led.

Each curve, each corner
You embrace
Will lead you
To your hiding place.

Inside your heart
Where you do roam
Your body knows its place
Called home.

GOD'S LOVE IS A MAGNET

People are people
They go on strange hikes
Beginning as children
On scooters or trikes.

They dream of travelling
On roads that are smooth
But the highway of learning
Is rough and rude.

People are people
They grow in slow spurts
In moments of weakness
In moments of hurt.

Looking for love
Without prickle or hook
They search for their answers
In every book.

Driving through life
To a dead-end stop
They meet up with farmers
Who lose their crop.

Learning from others
Who plant new seed
Their faith gets tested
In the hour of need.

Arriving at hunger
And longing to be fed
God's love is the magnet
By which they are led.

God's love is a magnet
That pulls and attracts
God's love is a magnet
That never attacks.

GHOSTS AND ANGELS

I've known rumblings
And the breakdown of the mind
And many times a death warrant
I've had to face and sign.

I've known earthquakes
And the crumbling of the land
And often in a crevice
I've been forced to take God's hand.

I've grown to know the landslides
And the rubble they leave behind
But underneath the tumult
This is what I find

A land with lovely landscapes
That a shattered woman found
When all her earthly longings
Had been buried in the ground.

A woman on a journey
Who fell before she rose
Who threw away her camera
Because she didn't want to pose.

A woman who is real
And doesn't fake her grin
A woman who has faced her ghosts
From deep down deep within.

A woman who's an angel
Because she's journeyed well
A woman who's been stricken
In heart, body, mind and cell.

A woman grown peaceful
Who soothes her feet with oil
Because the God who deeply loves her
Is lifting all her toil.

AWAKENED ARTIST

A painter scrubbing
Her canvas clean
Pastel is my colour
Soft and serene.

The dismal shades
Are in me, too,
Navy, black
And cobweb blue.

I hang my pictures up
With pride
But critics shove them
Far aside.

They scathe the cloth
On which I draw
And measure
Every kind of flaw.

I turn to Spirit
Take a breath
The work they stabbed
Gets put to death.

No longer needing
Human praise
A richer tapestry
I raise.

Lustrous colours
Brighter tones
My art gets chiselled
To the bone.

The Muse compels
My voice to speak
The artist in me
Cannot sleep.

ETERNAL WATERS

Down to the sea
I went today
No one to comfort
No one to play.

I threw myself
Onto the sand
Because I did not
Want to stand.

A child gone hungry
Without food for the day
My life, it seemed,
Had gone astray.

Heavy, weighted
Like a piece of lead
The God I worshipped
Had gone dead.

The ocean, now,
Seemed vast and wide
Without a place
For me to hide.

The waves rushed in
With sudden force
To turn me back
Upon my course.

Then drank I
Of a Water deep
That roused me
From my deadly sleep.

The eternal God
I now did taste
Uplifted by
Her living grace.

IMMORTAL MELODY

A sheet of music
I have it in my heart
I sing it most often
When alone and apart.

The sadness that's in it
Turns out to be joy
Like metals that mix
In pure alloy.

It happened this Song
The day that we met
Its melody never
Shall I forget.

As years went by
My memory faded
Because my music
Got berated.

Like tasteless food
Without any tang
My restless music
Crashed and banged.

The words, the notes
They seemed to flop
But never
Did my music stop.

Stale notes
And worn-out hymns
Gave way to new
And better things.

The poet in me
Found new zest
My music, then,
Was at its best.

COME PRUNER

Why the fruit
Do I pick from the tree
When yesterday
I could not see?

Why the bird
Do I hear it sing
When yesterday
I heard not a thing?

Why the flowers
In this land
When yesterday
I could not stand?

Why the grass
So green at my feet
When yesterday
It was dry with heat?

When I turn
These questions over
It's like the Pruner
Cutting clover.

One day the field's
Rich and green
And then, the shamrock
Goes unseen.

Should I live
Or should I die
That which is fallow
Will make me fly.

NO LONGER HIDING

Trying to win
But losing the race
I've worn a mask
To hide my face.

Others, too,
They wear a cloak
And crush the heart
Of human folk.

Defenses only
Make us weak
But still we play
Our hide and seek.

Like a beautiful sound
Within a bell
We long to break
This hidden spell.

Holding a scarf
Instead of a knife
What could this mean
In real life?

Removing the barnacles
From tired feet
And opening ourselves
To the stranger we meet.

Helping the man
Who walks with a cane
And loving the woman
Who frets and complains.

When living our life
Without wearing a hood
Life is a mirror
Reflecting the good.

WORLD REBORN

Where shall I look
Look looking find
People with whom
To share my mind?

Are these Spirit souls
On earth
Or must they still
Be brought to birth?

Has their vision
Swept the sky
Or has their ego
Not yet died?

In the blackest
Darkest night
Are their hearts
Still charged with Light?

Will there come
A time quite soon
When shadows cease
To clothe the moon?

Where people everywhere
Will see
God's glory shining
Bright and free.

DESERT LIFE

Learn of life
Before too late
The heart of a woman
Must learn to wait.

Seasons of dryness
She'll grow to despise
But seasons of dryness
Will make her wise.

She'll hate the yellow
Sterile things
The empty pain
That sorrow brings.

But out of it all
She'll come to know
An oasis that God alone
Can grow.

Fresh, pure water
Pollution free
God is the window
Through which she will see.

RIPENED SOUL

Have you ever been to a party
Where you feel like curdled milk
Because the dress you're wearing
Isn't really silk?

Oh, I've been to many a party
Where they treat you just that way
They smile as if you're pretty
But it's what they have to say.

My life has been that party
I've grown downward in my mind
But underneath the surface
This is what I find:

A garden far too lovely
My human mind to hold
And though I keep it hidden
One day it shall unfold.

My message has been brewing
Like yeast inside the dough
The leaven rising in me
Has taken years to grow.

My soul is filled with sunshine
My heart with deep content
And all that once was crooked
Is now no longer bent.

My food is rich and lavish
Like sweet, delicious bread.
Creation is God's energy
The love by which I'm fed.

SPIRIT LOVE

Like a breath of winter freshness
I saw a sunset in the snow
And looking down upon it
My heart was all aglow.

Each icy layer in me
Became a burning spark
And freed me from the terror
Of living in the dark.

My frozen bones now crackling
With warmth of sudden heat
Encircled every creature
That my living soul could meet.

I ran through every countryside
To spread what I had seen
But few there were who listened
To the Place where I had been.

The Love that grew inside me
Had wings that could take flight
And all that had been heavy
Turned into being light.

The hope that filled my being
Replaced my former fear
My journey now was simple
My pathway very clear.

The Spirit flowed within me
Like a fountain in the sky
And my soul that once was dragging
Was now lifted up on high.

POEMS FROM
FACE OF A GYPSY - 2007

"A religious sister, teacher, poet and Reiki Master, Eileen Curteis has followed a varied and unconventional spiritual path, ever-moving as in the mythology of the gypsy. Eileen's new risk-taking poems venture into the complex aspects of life and relationship. Although her work is resurrectional, she addresses with poignant clarity the fears and shadows of being human. In her accessible lyrical style, rich in visual imagery, Eileen the poet, invites you to jump on her caravan and travel with her on a journey inward."
　　Marnie Butler

"With refreshing honesty, Eileen Curteis takes pen in hand once again in this marvelous celebration of a life lived to its fullest. In a victory of spirit, Eileen dances to new rhythms in this latest collection of poetry. No facades here."
　　Claire Turcotte

"Here is work of disarming simplicity, the enigma of the obvious, news from the interior; here is an unashamed lyricism, which sings of spiritual discovery and renewal. If you seek poetry that is lambent, not merely clever, you will find it in this book."
　　Mike Doyle, Author of *Living Ginger* and *Intimate Absences: New & Selected Poems*

DARK-EYED FACE OF A GYPSY

Now that I have learned to accept
my own geography
nothing surprises me anymore -
fresh cream
on a sour potato
spoiled hamburger
on a rotten egg -
what does it matter
when the ingredients are you?

Are not each of us
born
raised
chosen
but how many would disclose
the vain wrinkle
in our weak world?

And how many
when the time comes
could look in a mirror and say:
"I see you, face of a gypsy,
dark eyes
black
as an untamed stallion
peering out at me,
peering out at you,
I see you, face of a gypsy."

THE WISDOM OF TORN SKIRTS

Roots in my cellar
and more roots
enough to cover me
from the shame of living here
but I am not ashamed.

Fighting for life
I've gone down under the brambles
held love like a lily
seen terror
the poisoned blackberry
cut me up like a thorn
cut me down like a tree.

I've seen death on the highway
flown into her like a blind bird.
Driving down wrong roads
in search of the right shore
for a girl to walk on
I've crossed over the bridge
called ugly
to embrace the goodness in me.

My torn skirts
have aged me considerably.

DANCING TO NEW RHYTHMS, LOST GIRLS
FIND THEIR WOMAN SOULS YOUNG AGAIN

Pushed down,
fallen,
under the weight of a mountain
sometimes North American girls
born into North American families
don't make it.

Their mothers say:
"Now dear,
you have everything
a third world child doesn't -
food, clothes, toys, games, money,
bracelets, earrings, necklaces -
everything a third world child doesn't!"

"Yes, mommy," they say,
"cock-a-doodle-doo!"
and go to bed hungry
as a chewed-up rooster.

You can't fool these girls.
They know
when a chocolate
turning over in its sleep isn't real.
Insipid as day old phlegm in the throat,
there is no substitute for love
when it goes down
like a sugarless candy.

Were you to ask these girls:
"What is a heart?"
they would cry,
"a bell clanging homesick
for its mother!"

Hankering for love
they could be the best girls
in the world
blowing their lungs out of a bugle
and still not be heard.

Driving uphill
into the new millennium
you may think there is no hope
for small girls on a scooter
grown big enough
to have the mouth of God in them
but look again.

Dancing sure-footed
you'll not find them tiptoeing
around a naked tree in winter.

As sure as God is
they'll come stomping
out of the kitchen
into a home
whose walls
can no longer confine them.

I FOUND MY POPPIES
OUTSIDE THE SYSTEM

I am a winter bird
that has no place
to lay its head.
I am winter all over
with a song in my heart
and no one to hear.

I sit on people's windows
pecking
at their closed-inness.
I sing
far beyond my strength
for the day
when they shall hear
and I will be gone.

Migrating south
I could be as present
as your finger is
or as anonymous
as my name has become.

A stranger at school today
nobody sees
the cavity called loneliness
in the desk where I sit.
Like a sliver of wood
I am too small
to be seen by anyone.

I have gone to this school
for twelve years now,
but I am too small
to be seen by anyone.

At university
I play the game called funeral.
Nobody attends the ceremony.
Only my books do.

Years later,
like sunshine
spurting out
from under the closed lid
of a coffin,
I kiss that stupid kid
in a wastebasket
better.

I'm a degreed person
who found her poppies
outside the system.

THE PAST IS PAST LARA

Fine features carved into a stone,
it was Lara's face that etched me in,
so many Lara's
so many knots tied up in a string,
a pain here, a canker there,
but why go on being Lara?

It's not good putting your face
in an empty bucket, Lara.
The past is past.
Gone, finished,
like white frost frozen
on the stump of a tree.

Change your name, Lara,
and with it
the grey jacket
zippered into your skin.

Freshen up a little
be a bubble bouncing on a ball
or try dancing barefoot
on a flattened shoe.

You can do it, Lara,
but remember
nothing is permanent
so why forecast anything.
Bad weather spelled backwards
in Africa
could be clear day in America.

SO MUCH TO HOPE FOR
WITH YOUR HAND IN MINE

I am not usually broken
but when I am
I need you
like wax in a candle
to melt into me.

With your hand in mine
I need you to say:
"I who have fallen
out of gaiety before
can embrace it again."

As much
as I should know
I am loveable
sometimes I don't.

That's why the link
of your arm in mine
has something to say
to all of us in desperation.

Something about
how we can't always be
on top of the stairs
and yet,
if somebody hopes in us
there's no saying
how high we will climb.

PORTRAIT OF A SOUL

I know you
though you speak
but little of yourself.

Sorrow
has silenced you
has made you gentle
and radiant.

Words —
they are no longer necessary.
I have only
to look in your eyes.

A TRIBUTE TO LIL

First of all, the eyes
blue enough to indulge in,
the ones your children inherited.

Gazing at you now
is like opening a book
wrinkled in time
knowing you as you were -
pure face
no cloud could hide,
no stone could shatter.

As gentle as you were
you rode through life
with the spirit of a stallion
and carried your duality well.

Washing the dishes,
scrubbing the floors,
putting meals on the table
you saw beauty in the ordinary
and we loved you for it.

I think God
must have been proud of you
when the mouth
of the blue sky opened
and you came sailing into our lives
not to charm, but to love us.

Perhaps that's the miracle
of motherhood.
You came like a beautiful clock
ticking your way into us.

You were just an ordinary mom
lighting a lamp
in dark places,
and now, dear mother,
of ninety-eight,
even if you tried to hide
your brightness
behind an eclipse of the moon
we would still find you shining.

Dear splendid butterfly
on bended wing
we will not hold you back
from your soaring
when the time comes.

Instead,
we'll gather the lilies,
and the scent
of your face
will be on them
fresh,
as if you never had
gone into hiding.

EVEN IN DEATH DAD'S LOVE WILL HEAL

Black,
colour of a torn-up tulip,
stick it on your father's face
until the eyes become indelible as yours.

Genealogy has it
the daughter inherits the look of her father.
One glance from these navy eyes
and she has the uncanny ability
to light up the dark corners
of a dim room.

They are so much alike,
father and daughter.
A small girl somersaulting down a hill
she exudes humour as freely as he does
only sometimes
she catches him playing
with dust balls in the thermos
as if there was something wrong
with growing old
something irreversible as bad breath.

She can't stop loving this man
he's the only dad she has
and she'd do anything to keep him forever
relinquish calendars, turn clocks backward
put him in her pocket
with a warm blanket marked
eternal daddy.

She remembers him as he was
huge heart
size of an ocean
forty years a school principal
loved, honoured, respected,
friend of children, parents
this beautiful man
falling off a pedestal
into a pit called no more
and she wants to save him.

Daddy's girl,
mischievous monkey,
they could be twins
in the same buggy
identical shoe laces
each going their separate way
he on one continent
she on another.

Long after he's gone
she'll remember her tiny hand in his
the big finger over the little one
tracing the word love
down the side of her cheek.

MORE PRECIOUS
THAN A TIMID DEER

We cherish those people
who cross our hearts
with the footprints of love.
My brother
is one of those people.

I had always known
and loved him
but for some strange reason
I loved him more that winter
than any other.

He called me by my name.
"Crushed snowdrop,"
he said,
"more precious than a timid deer,
you are loveable as anyone,"
and with that
the growth began.

That winter
for whatever reason
he held me
as if I never had been held,
loved me
as if I never had been loved.
My brother.

FUNKY GIRL
SMELLING THE FUNKY FLOWERS

It might be true
we're flourishing
as well as anybody
but sometimes
we're like weed and bramble
growing together.

Nobody says
we shouldn't be there
and, so,
we go on existing
not knowing
there's a better garden
elsewhere.

Sometimes
that's what getting
dug up means.
You end up
in different soil.

Trees, bushes, flowers,
people,
everything takes on
a new savour,
and what you get
is a taste
distinctively your own.

POEMS FROM
EXPOSED - 2018

"What makes the poems in *Exposed* unique is that I went back to my earlier art work of 1977 and allowed my soul to experience what the journey was like at age thirty-five. The small number of poems recorded here reflect that journey back in time."

    Eileen Curteis

"After forty-one years of incubation, Eileen's art has emerged and given birth to the poignant poetry and prose that so well describes both her and our delivery into this century. Exquisite and palpable, her work will live on forever."

    Stephanie Doucette

"The poems in *Exposed* are an intimacy of words, contributions from the soul, a voice from long ago which has waited for a time to be heard. This manuscript was Divinely inspired and Divinely gifted. From childhood experiences of loneliness and isolation to healing and joy, love and hurt, *Exposed* is a courageous metaphoric work that will touch the reader deeply, addressing issues with which we all can identify."

    Carey Pallister

"Eileen is not just a lovely woman I happen to know who explains her life through poetry; she is a true and serious wordsmith who I would not hesitate to place next to the poems of Goethe, the German novelist and poet."

    Judith Miller

OPENNESS

Brutal judgement
can stab a person open
but not in the journal
of this woman's life.

She takes an axe to it
bursts open the stone
and crushes it.

A bent woman
lying on the ground
you need
to be patient with her.

It takes time
for a house to crumble
before it falls,
time for the hard wood
to become pliable.

And even more time
for the clay body
of a woman
to push open
the lid that closed it.

PARADOX

Standing
on top of a broken bridge
you could be falling
into a chasm
and still not know
where you're going.

Up down
down up
an escalator
doesn't question
the route
the way we humans do.

We've got to go higher
up over the mountain
to the other side of day
to the place
where the dark face of God
lies hidden in the moonlight.

We need colour in our veins
turquoise blue and indigo red
we need to be children again
to paint the sky green
to live lavishly
before the day is over.

OCEAN SURVIVOR

Destined
for the higher seas
I was told
a small boat
travelling off course
will get you nowhere.

So, here I am
sitting on the edge
of a sinking ship
going down
into the basement
of the sea.

In this rudderless zone
you don't navigate
the ocean
it navigates you.

Losing control
even the waves stammer
become speechless
in your Presence.

If you are a loving God
and I know you are
I wish I could say
this is a dream I awaken from
unscathed, whole and complete
but I cannot.

FRAGILITY

When my petals open
you will see me
as I am
not as you
envisioned me to be.

Being dragged through
a field of dandelions
I could have told you
I would rot there
but you did not listen.

Turmoil
has been my teacher
has ripped me open
to tell you
a small girl
inside the shaking body
of a woman
lives here.

Hard as an acorn
fragility
has cracked me open
touch my petals
and you will see.

BELOVED MESSENGER

We may have skin
the colour of rainbows
but in our off season
we shut down
we of the brown,
the drab, the grey.

Falling into an abyss
of our own making
we the desolate ones
get chewed up by it.

Losing sight
of our homeland
we see the dark-faced One
coming toward us.

Even before her arrival
we know her Voice
will be the greening of us.

Picking a thousand daisies
we'd go anywhere
to follow her.

DAYBREAK

First ray of dawn
pressing in on me
that's who God is,
the hinge
behind the shut door
of my heart
prying me open.

Withered love
makes me thirsty
downcast in the rain
but you,
God of the morning
are not like that.

Dried up
you give me clean air
and a basin to wash in.

It doesn't matter
what road I take
even a detour
is travelling toward You.

Sitting
in a basket of thistles
or standing
on the horizon of a hill
nothing
will change
the way I love You.

GENTLE STRUM

Once sorrow
has plucked you
a home
your heart will sing
even as the lyre does.

If you run far from her
she will chase you
up a hill
put a ring on your finger
and say
marry me.

Only then
can Love
tilt your toes upward
spin you forward
into the pivotal dance
you came for.

Make sorrow
your melody
and she
will sing to you.

HEALING RAINSTORM

Out in the rain
the drenched face
mirrors
the drip within.

Soul cries out
no more space
in the wet room
of my heart
no more space.

Down the road
from where I live
people mimic my grief
they weep
as if stones
know how to do that.

Emotions
die
on the ground
in front of them.
I swallow them
whole.

Tears
and then
the prick
of a knife
sobs me open
sobs me free.

STRONGLY ROOTED

If your life becomes
an encyclopaedia
maybe you're on overload.
Try making it more succinct
a book with one chapter
instead of ten.

Now scrutinize your work
a script written
without a tear in the paper
tells only half your story.

That's why
a pencil
without an eraser
is the best way
to get to know yourself.

Mistakes are the springboard
to knowledge
erase them
and you deny
your journey.

Ask yourself:
Is your story
solidly rooted
or is it sitting
in a wheelchair
on the whim of another?

SPIDER WOMAN

In the circus of life
not every motion
will be good for you
so centre yourself
spider girl
and be strong
for the spinning.

Soaring too high, too fast
can be just as dangerous
as sitting in a stagnant pool
of passivity
when you should be
moving forward.

Sometimes
your best learning
will come in winter
when you
like the tragic whisper
in the mouth of a snowbird
have nothing to say.

In the end
if you can paint
on the canvass of your life
what it is to be whole
you will have achieved
what you came for.

FREE SPIRIT

If you think
holes in an umbrella
can stop the rain
from coming through
you're resisting something.

Duplicity maybe
or ignorance
where the wet mouse
goes on pretending
that she's dry.

Stop
this game playing
turn your eyes inward
under the parched skin
of your body.

And say
to your thermometer:
If I could take
your temperature now
you'd have to admit
God is the abyss
you are falling into.

Like her
love her
be drawn to her
as the only magnet
left living for.

SUN WOMAN

It's all about
bursting your bubble
breaking through the froth
of what it means
to be real.

If night is what
you've been living in
tell it
to the dark face
of the moon.

Now look at the sun
sitting behind the cloud
if she ever spoke
the way you do
you'd be disheartened
by her.

Glimpsing
beyond
the narrow field
of your smaller self
push the closed door
open.

Unzipper
that zippered heart
of yours.
A warm house
Is better than a cold one.

ECSTASY

One day
soul child was seen
carrying
a trinity of birds
in her knapsack.

The music was unseen
unheard
but definitely ethereal
and known
only to the listener.

From then on
whenever soul child
entered a house
the Energy in the room
became different.

Out of her feet
she could sprout wings
that made her fly.

In a body
physically close to you
she could be
wave lengths away
and still remain
intimate
as a cloud hugging you
after its spill of rain.

ABOUT THE AUTHOR

For the last 31 years, Eileen Curteis, a Sister of Saint Ann has been involved in the Reiki Healing Ministry, a revered eastern healing art that she combines with her Christian heritage of healing. A former teacher, principal and educator for 27 years, Eileen shares that her greatest passion now lies in her healing ministry and in the literary arts. She has authored fourteen books to date and has become an accomplished poet, artist and writer, as well as being a producer of seven CDs and three films. She lives in Victoria, BC.

Photo by Francis Litman

You can view Eileen's other books on
Amazon, Barnes and Noble and other
book retailers worldwide.

In this volume Eileen has not included poems from her more recently published books:

Mountain Mover, 2019, art and poetry.
Walk With Me Into The Light, 2022, art and poetry.